THE WARRIOR CODE

11 Principles to Unleash the
Badass Inside of You

THE
WARRIOR
CODE

TEE MARIE HANIBLE

WITH

DENENE MILLNER

ST. MARTIN'S PRESS
NEW YORK

www.stmartins.com

The Library of Congress Cataloging-in-Publication Data is available upon request.

ISBN 978-1-250-15672-3 (hardcover)
ISBN 978-1-250-15673-0 (ebook)

Our books may be purchased in bulk for promotional, educational, or business use.
Please contact your local bookseller or the Macmillan Corporate and Premium Sales
Department at 1-800-221-7945, extension 5442, or by email at
MacmillanSpecialMarkets@macmillan.com.

First Edition: February 2019

10 9 8 7 6 5 4 3 2 1

Dear Momma,

*So many things I wish I could say, conversations
I wish we'd had, moments I wish we could still share . . .*

Thank you for giving a lost little girl a place to call home.

CONTENTS

ACKNOWLEDGMENTS

Thank you to St. Martin's Press, especially to Denene, Monique, and Victoria for all your help and support. Thank you to RL Summers Photography Inc. for capturing what words never could. Thank you to my family for all your support and love over the years. I wouldn't be where I am without you. And lastly, to my beautiful, resilient, and smart mini mes, Destiny and Jasmine, thank you for making my job as a mom easier. I love you.

THE WARRIOR CODE

INTRODUCTION

No one is born a warrior. We don't come out of the womb with armor and weapons and the honor, courage, discipline, and strength to conquer life's toughest battles—to win the mightiest wars. That mettle—that ability to stare the enemy in the face, choose the right weapons, and fight with all one's might to survive—is learned and earned with time. With experience. With the knockdowns and the wherewithal to get back up again, no matter what, every time, having learned a little more about what it takes to do so, no matter how strong or cunning the opposition.

This is no easy task. That opponent is a sly one, for sure—not even, in most cases, a real person we can touch, see, or hit. Indeed, our biggest foe is not a person at all. It is, instead, all the things that hold us back from realizing our true strength and ability to win at life: fear, laziness, anger, ego, stubbornness, and so much more. Each threatens our greatest desires—that new job; true love; better connections with family and friends; stronger, fitter bodies; higher education; respect; stability—and brings the fight right to our doorstep. Directly to our hearts and minds. Neither knife, nor gun, nor fist is brandished, but this enemy can be every bit as lethal to us humans as an AK-47 with a full clip.

Being a true warrior, then, isn't so much about our ability to throw hands or shoot with precision or conquer adversaries we can actually see. It's about identifying our inner strength—tapping into the very core of our being to overcome the everyday obstacles that threaten to derail us at every turn. We all have the skill, knowledge, and muscle to get this done. Not only to endure but also to thrive—to be unbreakable.

I know this to be true because my life was not set up for survival. At least not an easy one. Before I'd even turned a year old, my father was shot dead in the street, my two-year-old brother crumpled at his feet. Not much longer after that, social services removed us from my mother's arms and dropped my brother and me into the complex, soul-sapping foster care system, leading to the Chicago home of a strict but loving couple that raised us in a whirlwind of poverty, old-school discipline, and a rotating crew of almost two dozen foster children in and out of their three-bedroom apartment. By age seventeen, I'd been kicked out of school, shot, piled into the back of several cop cars, handcuffed in a police interrogation room, awakened in a hospital bed after a drug-induced fainting spell, pregnant, and an active member of a dangerous gang. That I made it out of all of that is a miracle.

The military saved my life.

I survived the streets of Chicago, but becoming a Marine gave me my armor. Made me a warrior. At every turn, I proved myself as a woman and a single mother in the military, destroying every physical, mental, and emotional barrier to take my rightful place as one of the first women to serve in a male-dominated combat mission during Operation Enduring Freedom (OEF) / Operation Iraqi Freedom (OIF). So strong was my pull to defend my country, I deployed to Iraq—leaving behind my daughter, my family, my friends, and all I knew and loved to join my band of brothers on the ground. My work as a recruiter in the military as well as one of the Marines hand-selected to assist the Marine Corps in its mission to open combat roles to women paved the way for more strong women to join the military's elite. And after retiring from two decades of duty, I used my mix of tough love and Marine mettle to mentor everyday men and women on the hit Fox reality show *American Grit.*

When I consider where I've been and my journey to the right here and now, I know that every trial, every heartbreak, every decision—the good and the bad—every bullet made me the warrior I am today. Because I chose not to let the adversity I faced define or wreck me. I carried on.

I'm nobody's hero. I'm a woman. A mother. A daughter. A philanthropist. A Marine. A badass. A survivor. And I have a little something to say about what it takes to be a warrior. Pro tip: it's a lot more than muscle. Follow my journey in *Warrior* and you just might see that you, too, have what it takes to win your own personal wars.

—MARINE GUNNERY SERGEANT TEE HANIBLE

IMPROVISE, ADAPT, AND OVERCOME: GET SOME GRIT

THE WARRIOR CODE: PRINCIPLE #1

> *To be gritty is to keep putting one foot*
> *in front of the other.*
> *To be gritty is to hold fast to an interesting*
> *and purposeful goal.*
> *To be gritty is to invest, day after week after year,*
> *in challenging practice.*
> *To be gritty is to fall down seven times,*
> *and rise eight.*
>
> —*ANGELA LEE DUCKWORTH, ACADEMIC, AUTHOR*

Grit is perseverance—that passion we use to push through adversity, no matter the obstacles. That stick-to-itiveness. It comes wrapped in qualities like discipline, self-motivation, fearlessness, and a smidge of optimism. There's plenty of research that suggests that when it comes to achievement, having grit is as important as, if not more than, intelligence or talent. Ask any new Marine and they'll likely tell you the same: yes, of course you have to have brains and brawn to make it through the Crucible, the final physical evaluation that tests whether recruits have the physical, mental, and moral fortitude to be a Marine. But it's that grit—that dogged determination in your heart, in your sinew, in every fiber of your being—that gets you through fifty-four hours of food and sleep deprivation and forty-eight miles of marching while carrying forty-five pounds of gear as you work together to overcome obstacles, problem-solve, and help your fellow recruits ace the combat assault courses, the team-building and warrior stations, and the leadership reaction course. When your body is weak and your mind is tired and telling you, "Give up—you're not going to make it," it's that grit that kicks in and propels you forward and sees you through the end.

I believe we all have a bit of grit in us. It can reveal itself naturally, like in my case, when I had to lean on it to push through my challenging childhood, or it can be drawn out of us, like a bucket of water from a well when everything else in our lives has gone dry and we need the fortitude, the strength, the coping skills to quench our thirst and just keep pushing.

My grit was born, bred, and nurtured in the midst of childhood trauma. Before I took my first step, before I could even say my own name, the odds were against me. I was born in Chicago to a man and a woman whose troubles never gave them peace—that refused to give them rest. When I was just ten months old, that trouble found my father on a quiet street on the South Side, where he was walking with my big brother, a chocolate dewdrop still in diapers, tottering on the pavement alongside our dad. Quick as a flash, someone walked right up to the two of them, pulled out a gun, and shot my father dead. Just left his body—crumpled, bloody—right there in the middle of the street, with my brother standing over him, screaming. From what little information I've managed to gather over the years, my brother wasn't hurt, but beyond that, I have no idea if the person who killed my father was ever found, arrested, or punished.

This was the beginning of the end of our family and the tragic start to my life.

Not long after, I'm told, child services showed up at my mother's door, packed up my brother and me, and piled us into the back of a car—drove us away from our mother, away from our home, away from the only family and life we'd ever known. Promises were exchanged: if she got herself together, child services told my mother, she could get her babies back; the moment she got herself together, my mother told child services, she would get her babies back. Those were promises never kept.

Instead, my brother and I ended up in the care of Minnie and William Hudson, an older couple who made a tacit agreement to house, clothe, feed, and love on us—to do all the things our mother simply could not and would not do. They kept a home on the South Side, not too far from where my brother and I had been living—a tiny, crammed, three-bedroom apartment that held court for a rotation of children numbering anywhere from two to twenty at any given time, sleeping on the couch, the floor, sometimes three or four to a bed. The two of them were the only parents I'd ever known, and their ragtag collection of foster care children would become my de facto extended family, a group of children who did not carry the same blood as I but who stood in as sisters and brothers and play cousins and even mothers when I needed that nurturing touch—the touch that I never again got from my birth mother, who, despite promising to visit my brother and me, never came to see us. There were many visits from

social services caseworkers checking up on our well-being
and offering counseling, but never, ever did my birth mother
darken the threshold of the Hudsons' door, much less step
back into her role as our caretaker, as the mother who gave
birth to two children and dedicated herself to feeding
us, clothing us, loving us, praying over us. The magnitude
of this was devastating, as it would be, I'd imagine, for any
child aching for her mother's kiss, her mother's touch. I was
consumed with wondering where my mother was, what she
was doing, why she didn't come for me. If she loved me.
Mrs. Hudson, then still my foster mother, never minced
words when I asked the questions: from the moment I was
able to understand the words coming out of her mouth, she
told me all she knew about how we'd come to live with her,
and when she got updates on my mother's whereabouts and
living situation, she made a point of letting me know, too.
The more I was able to understand the gravity of my mother's
actions, the more I was able to chart her absence, the larger
the hole in my heart grew. That emptiness was compounded
by the news that, at some point, she got pregnant again and
had a baby girl—a child, I assumed, she kept and cared for
on her own. There I'd be, cuddled up next to my brother in
a tiny corner of our bed, staring at the ceiling, listening to
the rhythm of his breath and wondering where this new
little sister was—if she was cuddled up next to my mother at
that very moment, what their room looked like, why my
mother loved her enough to raise her but not even check up
on me. Eventually, my adopted mom would tell me that my
little sister wasn't in my birth mother's care at all—that she
gave up that baby, too, and she was being raised by our

grandparents. Knowing this tore me to pieces, too; my grandparents loved my little sister enough to take her in, but not my brother and me. We were beasts of no nation. I was a motherless child.

But Minnie Hudson was there for me. She stepped into that empty space.

Momma was a grandmotherly type—the kind of no-nonsense woman who, typical of her generation, thought children should be seen and not heard. She and Dad were already well into their sixties when my brother and I arrived, and by the time I hit double digits, they looked old enough to be my grandparents. When I close my eyes and picture her, my mind always zooms to me as a little girl, playing skellies and jacks and jumping rope with the other neighborhood kids, my forehead sweaty, pigtails flying, breathing heavily, hard at play, when she steps out the front door of the apartment building and calls us inside for dinner. Always, she's in a housecoat, like the very embodiment of Tyler Perry's iconic Madea character from the movies: gray-haired, larger-than-life, older, brash, stern. A bit embarrassing. It would nearly kill me to turn toward her voice and see her standing there, her hand on her hip, that same housecoat clinging to her body, waving us into the house for dinner. All I could do was hang my head and scurry inside, hoping everyone would honor the code that it's not acceptable to talk about anyone's mama.

I wouldn't have tolerated that anyway. Minnie Hudson loved me in the best way she knew how: by providing for me. She didn't have much outside the checks she got from the state to care for us kids, but she stretched every penny to make sure we kids had exactly what we needed. We weren't the Cosby family living in a brownstone, wearing expensive sweaters, sitting in a well-appointed living room talking about jazz music and which fancy college we'd attend—not even a little bit. Even the simplest things were out of reach: there were no Friday night family bowling trips or Sunday treks to the Riverwalk or family dinners at a favorite deep-dish pizza spot. I can remember going to the movies only twice in my childhood, including once when my older sister Patricia took her daughter, Nichole, to see *ET* and let us tag along.

Even more challenging was adapting to the emotional instability of being a child in the system. When you're a foster child, you embrace disappearing—get comfortable rather quickly with becoming an inanimate object. Your lot is clear and the consequences of stepping outside the boundaries are practically scrawled in blood across the proverbial wall: your foundation is shaky and could crumble beneath your feet at any moment if you step out of line or show yourself to be a burden, which could result in your being sent off to a new foster care home or, worse, a group home, where your safety and survival is almost always tested. I wanted to be the kept child—the one my foster parents didn't send away.

That was always the fear—that if I didn't mind my business or I was too much trouble or my brother acted out, we'd be sent away. It's not what we were told, mind you. But we'd witnessed kids coming and going, and I don't know about my brother, but I was scared. Of course, because I was so young and no one told me differently, I didn't know that when a foster kid left my then-foster parents' home, that child was to be reunited with the birth parents who'd worked hard to get their children back. In my child's mind, foster children who acted out got the ultimate punishment: a precarious living arrangement even more unstable than the one they were living in already.

I witnessed this up close repeatedly. The foster kids who came through my then-foster parents' home weren't there for only a short spell; they'd stay until their families got back on their feet—six months, a year. Some of them would be my age; we'd go to school together, play and eat and sleep together, tell the kids in our class, "Oh, that's my cousin," or, "That's my stepbrother," or whatever title we could think of to explain the new kids and where they came from. We'd make up fantastic tales about where they were from and how they were visiting the house for a while—whatever we could pass off as the truth without having to actually tell the truth.

But when they left, another hole would get hammered in my heart, ripping off the scab that covered over my issues with abandonment. The one that hit me the hardest was Caroline. She was my sister through adoption—a girl my parents took into their home and raised for years. But she was so sad and angry about her circumstances; she wanted desperately to be back with her birth family, and she resented our adopted mother for taking her in and legally turning her into a Hudson. In Caroline's mind, our adoptive mother broke up a potential reunion with her birth mom. Before the ink could dry on her adoption papers, Caroline was plotting an escape: she was going to run away and find her blood mother and father, and she decided who would help her.

"I'll pay you five dollars," Caroline said, cornering me outside our apartment building one afternoon while she, Nichole, and I were playing. She was dedicated to the cause and wanted to make sure I was, too. "I'm going to write a note, and all you have to do is tell her you found it under your Cabbage Patch doll and give it to her. Can you do that?"

I was about age six and just happy to be with the big girls. But really, I didn't want Caroline to go. She was my sister; I looked up to her, and she was kind to me. I thought I took up the same space in her heart, but her birth family had a magnetic pull on that muscle. She needed to be with them more than she loved being with me. She wanted out.

A few weeks after she hatched her plan, Caroline made her move. She kissed my cheek and cupped my chin. "Be good, you hear?" she said. And with that, I watched her as she tossed a small duffel bag filled with her things out the porch window and climbed out after it.

I cried for the longest time after she left. But even at that tender age, I understood why she had to leave. I didn't necessarily agree with it; I never resented my mother for adopting me, but I did resent my situation. Eventually, I came to hate that my birth mother left my brother and me there to fend for ourselves—to have to be those kids with no history, no bloodline, no connection to our ancestors.

This was most acute every year when we had to do the obligatory family tree assignments and other classwork that involved revealing details about our birth, parents, and homelife. I hated it. It was the bane of this adopted child's existence—sitting there in a classroom with clammy hands, waiting to show off a poster full of lies, pretending that my birth parents never existed, wishing I had the real details of my lineage—that the leaves in my tree knew me and I knew them and the blood that ran through my tree's roots reached deep inside of me and made my leaf as rich and strong and vibrant as the leaves on my classmates' family trees. But I didn't have that; it was an impossible, impossibly insensitive assignment that made me feel like a loser. Already, I was embarrassed because my parents were older, and every time they came to the school for family events, the questions flew: "Is that your granny? Why are your parents so old?" It only got worse when those family tree assignments came along, and the teachers and counselors would work with my mom to help me work through the trauma and grief of being unable to complete the assignment, making me stand out even more. Every time the assignment came, I would get the worst case of anxiety; I'd be sitting at the kitchen table, staring at the paper, my pencil poised over the empty spaces as tears streamed down my cheeks. My now-adoptive mother did her best to try to make me feel better about it, but what I preferred was to not do the assignment at all. Alas, the teacher wasn't about to change the entire assignment for an entire class of thirty kids because one kid had a problem with it, so I'd do the best I could, which, in my book, was never—could never—be enough.

I was desperate to know in which direction my blood flowed, but it wasn't something that I spoke about out loud, because I didn't want to insult my adoptive mother—didn't want her to think that I didn't appreciate all that she had done for me or recognize that my birth mother had failed me in ways that my adoptive mother had not. I did pour out my feelings on the page, though, in a book I penned for a young authors competition at my school. It was called "Why Me," about a girl who struggled with being adopted and not knowing where she truly came from. In my story, the birth mom came back, only to have to navigate her daughter through a series of emotions—love and hate the strongest among them—as they reconnected and forged a new bond.

The book made it through the district competition and actually went to state competition, but I missed it because there was no one to take me. I was sorely disappointed—a familiar refrain in my childhood. But I never told anyone.

It was more important that I keep my head down. To stay as silent as possible. Because the last thing I wanted was to be a burden—a child who was seen and heard. More than any information I could have ever gleaned about my birth mother, what I needed most was to be kept around. In my child's mind, doing so was about survival.

I'm not going to lie: recounting the emotional and physical trauma of my childhood is not an easy thing. There is a lot of pain there—the kind that's so white hot and sears so deeply that I didn't even realize when it was happening that it was actually hurting me. But this was my way as a child—indeed, the way of all-too-many children who deal with trauma: we go through the fire and hold in the screams because yelling out could expose us, make us a visible target.

This is a lot like what it's like on an actual battlefield: we are trained to avoid detection, a skill that, behind enemy lines, could mean the difference between successfully evading capture and becoming a prisoner of war. We're taught, among many other things, specific skills, like how to move silently while crossing terrain, keeping snow and leaves from crunching beneath our feet, and how to move with the wind so that the sounds of nature mask the noise of our legs swishing or our gear jiggling as we slip around trees and up hills and through fields with foliage swaying in the breeze. We're also taught, in the face of great pain, to swallow our cries because one shriek, one yelp, one small screech could alert the enemy to our position and get us killed. Though we go to combat ready to die, we warriors on the battlefield keep a laser-sharp focus on both our mission and staying alive.

It is about survival.

What needs to go hand in hand with survival, though, is resiliency—grit. We have to have the ability to stand tall, get tough, and persevere after life knocks us down. So many of us suffer from real trauma: physically abusive parents or partners; poverty and its effects on our ability to have the basics, like food, shelter, and a safe environment in which to grow; toxic work environments; drug and alcohol dependency that further unravels our ability to physically, mentally, and emotionally cope. But the true mark of a warrior is being able to pull yourself out of the muck that the trauma causes in your life and move on with it.

I'm not suggesting for a second that you dismiss the pain. Feel that. Let it burn. But then grab your first aid kit, put some salve on it, wrap it, and let it heal. Learn from it. And vow to make it so that whoever comes behind you doesn't have to feel that same pain. As a child, I survived the emotional turmoil of living in a home where my stability—the very ground on which I put one foot in front of the other—was constantly shifting and moving. Uncertain. I wasn't sure from one day to the next if the knock on our apartment door was my birth mother coming to claim me, or if the kid I was sleeping next to and calling my sister would be gone tomorrow, or if that little thing I did that all kids do would earn me a whupping I'd spend weeks trying to forget. But each one of these experiences ultimately made me hardy. They didn't break me. Looking back at all that I went through as a child, I can still see the good there. I can also recognize that the trauma helped me develop an extremely thick emotional skin that helped me soldier through some difficult moments in my life: getting pregnant as a teen, witnessing extreme violence in my neighborhood, getting kicked out of high school, leaving my daughter to answer the call of duty overseas, three failed marriages. My survival through each of these things and so much more was dependent on grit. And I came out the better for it.

So how do you get yourself some grit, even and especially if it doesn't come naturally to you?

STARE DOWN YOUR FEARS. When faced with something that feels absolutely insurmountable and scares the mess out of you, don't turn your head away from it. Instead, acknowledge you're scared, figure out the reasons why this is so, then come up with a rational plan for how to overcome that fear. For example: the very thought of making a speech in front of an audience of strangers can send some people into a full-on panic. To build up your grit, accept the invitation to give remarks at your company's annual retreat, then get yourself prepared by thinking about what you're going to say, writing down your key points—or your entire speech—then practicing it alone and then in front of a trusted group of people before you present it at the retreat. By the time you're standing in front of your colleagues, you'll have that fear licked.

I know—easier said than done. But life is full of high-stakes situations that become all the more stressful when you approach the task thinking about all the ways something can go wrong. Besides, failing won't kill you; it'll make you feel bad, sure, but on the other side of it, you'll only get better, stronger. You might even learn from your mistakes and try again with that new knowledge—the kind of knowledge you need to actually turn your effort into success. I think Winston Churchill said it best: "Success is not final, failure is not fatal: it is the courage to continue that counts."

BE SELF-RELIANT. Of course, it's always great to be surrounded by people willing to lend a helping hand, but no one is going to put his or her back into meeting your personal goals like you will. This is something you learn fairly early when growing up in challenging circumstances. If I wanted something but I knew my mother didn't have the money to get it for me, I found a way to get it for myself. Now, I may not have always gone about it the right way; stealing coats out of lockers, wearing my sister Nichole's clothes without asking, and taking some other things that didn't belong to me weren't the right ways to go about getting what I wanted, but I did learn fairly early on that if my heart desired it, I had to go get it, because waiting for it to be handed to me wasn't an option. There was a safety net for families like mine, sure, but it was frayed by politics and a lack of resources, a combination that leaves mothers to struggle, children to go hungry, and communities to crumble. If you wanted to eat, you needed a roof over your head, you had to have a little money in your pocket to make it from day to day, you had to depend on yourself.

I know this sounds like a "pull yourself up by the boot-straps" argument, but that's not what I'm suggesting here. I truly believe it is our collective responsibility as humans to support fellow humans who are incapable of being self-sufficient, meaning they neither have nor have access to resources for basic care. But when you are self-reliant, you take responsibility for being the sole agent of your development and survival. You know the saying, "Give a man a fish and he'll eat for a day, but teach a man how to fish and he'll eat for a lifetime"? That's what I'm talking about: learning how to fish so that you can sustain yourself, even in times when others are incapable or unwilling to help you.

I've learned that the only person I can truly depend on is me, and I know that no matter how difficult the circumstance, I can find a way to make it through by remembering home and acknowledging and truly understanding how far I've come and knowing, for sure, every single component I had to call on to be the Tee Marie I've become. I'm not ashamed of who I used to be; she was an incredibly important piece of my life puzzle. But I came to know that growth was possible. Necessary.

BE OPTIMISTIC. In every cloud there is a silver lining, but you won't see it if you're constantly waiting for the rain to fall. Focus on the things that bring you joy and know, for sure, that trouble doesn't last always. Think about it this way: I failed my first rifle range qualification—couldn't do what needed to be done to pass muster when it came to the rigors of showing I had what it took to be a Marine. I could have given up, dropped out of basic training, and gone back to

Chicago with my tail between my legs. But I didn't. Instead, I called on my grit to go for it a second time, and I had faith enough in my physical, mental, and emotional abilities to go harder the second time around and ace what I had to do to pass the test and become a Marine. I knew I could do it, I envisioned myself doing it, and I did it.

GET BACK UP—EVERY DAMN TIME. Life is full of moments that knock the veritable wind out of us. You can either lie there and wallow and agonize over what's happened to you, or you can stand back up, dust yourself off, and keep going. This is that bounce-back: you can fall and get back up bouncing on your toes. No matter what gets lobbed like a Molotov cocktail your way, you adapt in the face of things that threaten to tear you to pieces: family problems, issues with your mate, a boss that drives you batty, a toxic workplace with coworkers who make it their personal business to sabotage you, even serious health problems. In my case, getting back up came in the form of being kicked out of school and, instead of dropping out, going to military school and doing what I had to do to earn my diploma. I had to prove to my family and especially to myself that I had what it took to buck the low expectations of others and graduate—make something of myself when everyone else saw nothing but the worst in me. No matter how many times life knocked me down then and knocks me down now, it is like the famous poem by my favorite writer, Maya Angelou, in which she brags, "Still I Rise." The grit is the part you call on to get back on your feet. You got this.

WARRIOR WORK

List three life challenges you've faced, plus how you perse-
vered.

_____

_____

_____

_____

_____

_____

_____

_____

_____

_____

_____

_____

_____

_____

_____

_____

_____

_____

List a tough challenge you're facing now. What scares you most? What can you do, right now, to dig in and develop a plan to fix it? List the steps to that plan.

_____

_____

_____

_____

_____

_____

_____

_____

_____

_____

_____

_____

Grit is not just a simple elbow-grease term for rugged persistence. It is an often invisible display of endurance that lets you stay in an uncomfortable place, work hard to improve upon a given interest, and do it again and again.

—SARAH LEWIS, CULTURAL CRITIC

2

UNCOMMON VALOR: GET TOUGH

THE WARRIOR CODE: PRINCIPLE #2

> *You're going to go through tough times—that's life.*
> *But I say, "Nothing happens to you, it happens for*
> *you." See the positive in negative events.*
>
> —*JOEL OSTEEN, PREACHER*

Being tough is not to be confused with being strong, with bulging muscles and brute strength. One is about being strong enough to toss someone across a room; the other is being tough enough to get back up again after being tossed across a room. One requires physical strength while the other requires mental tenacity. The latter is the one you want in your warrior arsenal.

See, being mentally tough means you won't crumble at the slightest provocation or even under the harshest circumstances. What does that look like? Think Michael Jordan scoring thirty-eight points in the Chicago Bulls' pivotal Game 5 against the Utah Jazz in the 1997 NBA Finals. Jordan was suffering from either the flu or food poisoning, and in the first quarter of the game, he was so dehydrated and exhausted he actually staggered on the court. But he insisted on playing through the illness because his team needed him; losing wasn't an option in a seven-game series that was tied 2–2, and Jordan knew that without his best effort, the Bulls' shot at winning both the game and the series was greatly diminished. By the time he hit his last three in the fourth quarter, clinching the win, fellow teammate Scottie Pippen had to hold up Jordan as he made his way off the court. For his part, Jordan said playing through the illness was "probably the most difficult thing I've ever done. I almost played myself into passing out just to win a basketball game." For us Chicagoans, his effort was nothing short of epic.

Jordan was an athlete, sure, with the conditioning and prowess to be a champion player. But his mental toughness, the kind that could help him push past a debilitating illness to win a high-stakes championship game, is what makes him a legend.

That same mental toughness is sown in the fabric of Chicago, my hometown. Of course, these days when one mentions Chicago, it's to rag on it, particularly the neighborhoods in which I grew up. It's not uncommon for my city to be referred to as *Chi-Raq*, the American answer to war-torn Iraq. I hate the term, but I understand the sentiment behind it: gun violence in our streets is every bit as treacherous as it was when I was a kid there—if not worse. And high unemployment rates, increased poverty, a depressed housing market, a police force that was found to have preyed on minority communities and the most vulnerable living in them, a broken educational system, government corruption, and so much more have all conspired to cripple Chicago and its once solid reputation of being one of America's premier cities.

But look closer: Chicago is more than the sum of its problems. It is a city whose people—and their very humanity—deserve more than finger wagging and tongue clicking. Growing up there, I saw how the streets tried to break people—children in particular. I saw the effects of poverty up close—kids wearing the same dirty clothes to school four weeks straight because those were the only clothes they had and no one had money or soap powder or washing machines, and kids at school exchanging food stamps for a couple quarters so they could get something to eat at lunchtime, the only meal they'd get all day. Like Langston Hughes says in his poem, "Mother to Son," life for me ain't been no crystal stair, but we were most certainly more comfortable than some of the kids who sat next to me in class and the lunchroom. Seeing this up close as a child made me appreciate my own circumstances a bit more, sure, but as an adult, when I consider how we kids soldiered through this madness, I have to give thanks for those of us who made it to the other side. I'm certainly better able to understand how complicated and fragile life can be, particularly for children who neither asked to be here nor had the tools to do better. Be better. It is so much clearer to me how all of these things manifest themselves in destructive ways and the kind of toughness it takes to not only physically, mentally, and emotionally survive it but also use the experience as a tool for greater good.

Hot, sticky days were made for toughness—and trouble—in the streets of Chicago. That's all we ever found on "the 9," our nickname for Seventy-ninth Street, the two-and-a-half-mile block that stretches between five different neighborhoods and several gang territories on the South Side. Today, the local media refers to it as "Murderers' Row," a fitting title considering the sheer amount of violence that ricochets like bullets up and down the block. I look at that street today and know nothing much has changed there: the 9 was just as dangerous way back when I was a fast-tailed teenager, shoving crinkled ten-dollar bills into the hands of bums who made the sidewalk their home, promising them they could keep the change if they scored some St. Ides or Mad Dog 20/20 for my fellow underage friends and me. We'd just walk up and down that road, drinking and laughing and flirting with boys. It was all good, red-blooded American teenager fun until the bodies dropped—until your friend was there one day and gone the next. That's the way it went down on the 9: somebody would get popped, and we'd creep down there to see who it was, fingers crossed, hoping with the might of the angels that whoever was on that stretcher or in that ambulance or outlined with that chalk wasn't somebody we knew. I was fifteen years old when my friends—many of them not even twenty yet—started being counted among the dead. I'd see their mothers crying on the news or, worse, I'd witness the overwhelming grief in person, the red and blue flashes of the police lights dancing across their faces, their cries drowned out by the sirens. Always, we would stand there, silent, numb, sure of everything and nothing at all. Everyone dies—that is life. Why did they have to die? This ain't living.

We thought ourselves tough because somehow we would just bury the dead and the pain that came with the loss, head to the school auditorium to hear the requisite counseling lectures the school sociologist was required to give the student body whenever a fellow student died, drag ourselves back to our boring classes, and then, after school, make ourselves feel good the best we knew how: by drinking and smoking the pain away. I remember being near inconsolable when one particular friend of mine was killed; once they got the news, all my girls from Ninety-third Street drove over to my neighborhood to pick me up so we could say goodbye. I climbed into that car with them without hesitation; with them, I could find solace. With them, I could be me. Snuggled between two warm bodies in the back seat, I let my tears flow as we drove through the streets of Chatham, somber. Angry. We ended up at a friend's house and lay out all over the living room furniture, drinking liquor like we were adults. Coping the only way we knew how.

We were just a bunch of kids—rebellious, thickheaded—and, to us, the fighting, the killing, the slow singing and flower bringing that came as regularly as the rising of the tide were as normal and expected as the shine of the sun. That's the way it was in Chicago when I was growing up. The way it is right now. Destructive. Normal. Expected. Everybody was clear that somebody was going to get popped and die and we friends would have to, once again, band together and cry and drink our way through the hurt, and then we'd all take our butts home, go to sleep, and wake up and go to school and start the entire cycle all over again.

Then came the day when the bullet had my name on it.

We'd been out on the 9 for hours, doing what we did, when someone crept up on us and started shooting indiscriminately into the crowd. There was no warning. There was no fight that served as a precursor to the mayhem. Just shots ringing out and feet scattering and bottles dropping and girls screaming and complete and utter chaos. Instinctively, I ran, heart racing, legs moving as fast as I could get them to move toward some kind of barrier or shelter, but really, there is no out-running bullets. If it wants you, it'll get you. And this one was mine.

The pain was sharp, searing—a hurt I'd never before known coursing through my inner thigh. I grabbed at the wound in disbelief. "Oh my God, I got shot!" I yelled out, falling to the pavement. My friends rushed over and frantically pulled me behind a car, the entire time screaming and grabbing and asking me where I'd been hit. The blood oozing through my fingers betrayed my wound—a graze that tore through my jeans and flesh.

"We have to get her out of here!" one friend yelled.

The moment the bullets stopped and we all thought it safe enough to move, my friends piled me into a car and drove frantically to a squat, dirty house where a local crackhead lived. All of us knew we'd be reasonably safe there, and plus, there was a nurse there who could help me. Going to a hospital, after all, was not an option. Neither was calling my mother or older sisters. Gangbanging, underage drinking, getting shot—all those things were the worst offenses any one teen could commit, and I'd achieved the trifecta all in one evening, due solely to a long list of bad decisions. *If this bullet doesn't kill me first, they will*, I remember thinking.

And then I passed out.

I was in and out of consciousness at the crackhead's house, but the nurse assured me I'd make it. The bullet grazed my leg—it didn't go all the way through—and outside of the blood loss, I wasn't too bad off, she said. While my friends washed my jeans, the nurse patched me up, gave me instructions for changing the dressing on my wound, and left me there to recuperate enough to get myself home. I was there until seven o'clock the next evening, completely unaware that my family, frantic over the fact that I'd been missing for well over twenty-four hours, had canvassed the local hospitals, called the police, and filed a missing child report. When I finally called my sister Dorothy, her voice was tinged with a mix of elation, relief, and anger.

"Where are you?" she demanded.

"I'm near Eighty-seventh Street," I said, deliberately avoiding giving her an exact address. I didn't want her to bring any trouble to the crackhead or the nurse who'd helped me. "Can you come get me?"

"Tee, we were worried sick about you. What have you been doing all night?"

I met her question with silence. Then, finally, I asked her again, "Can you pick me up?"

I limped to where I asked my sister to meet me, and about fifteen minutes passed before I was climbing into the front seat of Dorothy's car, wearing someone else's jeans, with a massive number of bandages hiding the truth of what'd happened just the night before. Dorothy was yelling the whole way home, demanding to know where I had been and assuming I was with some boy. I kept it simple: "I was with my friends."

Before we could get into the front door, she gave me the worst whupping I'd ever gotten in my entire life, plus a promise that the next time I disappeared and failed to let my mother or her know where I was, she would call my cousin Sonya, a Chicago police officer, and have her lock me up.

That was my life, but it wasn't what my mother wanted for

me—not the way she raised me. Honestly, though, she was no match for the streets of Chicago. Up until I hit the end of elementary school, the trouble I got into was mostly minor. I ran away once after getting suspended from school for fighting; I spent the afternoon after school in the park trying to think of a master plan to escape my mother's extension cord and ended up running to my aunt Ollie's house because even though my mom and Aunt Ollie were alike in many ways, I knew Aunt Ollie always had a soft spot for me and my brother; she would never raise so much as a finger to hurt me. That was about as wild as I got. But what I ended up learning on the streets changed me. I was a sponge to my environment. What I learned there became my gospel, and by age fifteen, I was totally uncontrollable.

What I wanted was attention. My brother was sucking up all of it on his own, albeit for reasons that were quite negative. His grades sucked, and every time he got a bad report card or a teacher sent home a telltale note outlining just how poorly he was doing in class, he got lectures, beatings, punished—interaction. Human connection. I brought home great grades in honors courses and held grade-wide top academic standings in elementary school and, in my mind, all I got was "hand me a pen so I can sign your report card." No one seemed to feel good or bad about my work—just indifferent. The silence was deafening.

And so I sought that attention elsewhere. I lost my virginity just shy of two weeks before my sixteenth birthday. The guy I was seeing was twenty-two. In my fifteen-year-old mind, it made sense to give it to him because all my other friends were doing it and being promiscuous was something you did without thinking twice about it. Indeed, it was my wanting to be grown and my gang affiliation, and especially my loyalty to the gang in my old neighborhood, despite going to school in rival gang territory, that got me in the most trouble. That trouble started the moment I left for the school bus in the morning. I'd kiss my mother good-bye and walk out the door in one outfit, and before I got out the front door of our apartment building, I'd have changed into a totally different outfit—usually some name-brand clothes I'd boosted from Nichole's closet. Her mother, my sister Patricia, gave birth to her and left her with my mother, who used to shower Nichole, whom I called my sister, with all kinds of gifts—especially fancy clothes and shoes. Because my mother was on a limited income, she had to make her social security dollars stretch, so my closet was full of clothes and shoes from the Dollar Store and Payless. My mother believed in us wearing those clothes until they were thread-bare, too; even if our shoes were full of holes and talking while we walked, we couldn't get new ones until the sole completely separated from the actual shoe. There was no way I, as a teenager, could survive the wrath of fellow students while wearing Dollar Store clothes and flapping shoes, so I would raid Nichole's closet and rock her Girbaud jeans and Cross Colours shirts, and squeeze my feet into her LA Gear sneakers. By the time I'd get to first period, I'd look like a completely different person, slumped at a desk in the back of the classroom with an outfit I didn't own, a face full of makeup, and an attitude. Being smart didn't matter anymore. Being down did. Later in the day, a few others and I would ditch school altogether and hide in the building's nooks and crannies. My school, Chicago Vocational High School (CVS), was said to have been built in the 1940s, during World War II, so in keeping with the time in which it was built, the school had multiple underground passageways and tunnels throughout it, so it was never hard to find a place to dip off to whenever someone had snuck some liquor or weed into the building.

By sophomore year, my gangbanging was leading to some serious repercussions. I had my clique of friends—a group of people with whom I hung out both because I liked them and because there was safety in numbers—and we tore all through that school, which, by then, had gotten so overrun by bad behavior and ineffective leadership that there were shootings, literally, in the hallways and on campus. Soon enough, we were walking through metal detectors to get to class, and I was scrapping with anyone and everyone who so much as looked at me funny. I spent my fair share of time in the principal's office, getting punished for my bad behavior. But that was lightweight stuff. I found my real trouble in the lockers.

We called it *locker scavenging*. The police? They called it *theft*.

Of course, it was easy to do, until it wasn't. Every security guard had a master key to the lockers, and only they were supposed to use it to open the lockers of students who couldn't get to their belongings. But if they trusted you, and they were feeling particularly lazy that day and didn't feel like making the long haul all the way across campus and up the stairs to your locker, all you had to do was ask and they'd let you take the key and go open your own locker, so long as you brought the key back to them. Those of us who knew what was up would ditch class, get our hands on the key, grab all our friends, and go from locker to locker, looking for things—coats, shoes, money—to steal.

We were collecting some pretty nice hauls, too, until the one day when I stole a Triple F.A.T. Goose down coat and got busted. The person to whom it belonged snitched, and the administration turned my crew and me over to the police. One would think that being paraded down the hallways in handcuffs and slammed into the back of a squad car would be scary—embarrassing. But I was a total badass—full of attitude and too ridiculous to be afraid. They got me down to that police station, and all I could do was laugh. Here were these cops—police officers I'd been taught all my life by the streets to hate because no one believed they meant us well—and they were in my face, threatening and trying to scare me. I blew them off with my humongous attitude, telling myself that I hadn't done anything more wrong than what I'd seen others do in that school, including the security guards, some of whom were having sex with students and others who were selling drugs. Those guards knew what was up. If I went down, I thought, they were going to go down, too.

Sometime around 7:00 P.M., after spending all day at the station, my sister Dorothy finally showed up and rescued me. I don't know what she said to get me out of there or so that I could escape charges, but I was relieved she came. That had to be the longest car ride ever.

Dorothy went in. "What the hell were you thinking?" she yelled.

Soon enough, I'd tuned her out, my attitude too big to care

that she was upset or that I could have gotten into much more serious trouble.

That wouldn't be my only time in the back of a squad car. On another occasion, I was detained for being out after curfew—even though I was at a friend's Fourth of July birthday party, literally right across the street from my apartment building. Yet another time, I was detained for fighting. The police hadn't actually caught me in the act of throwing hands with another girl, mind you; they'd caught me walking away after the big brawl. Because they couldn't prove I'd actually fought, eventually, they let me go.

I was such a badass—my life spiraling out of control, with no safeguards to keep me from going completely off the rails. And finally, after the arrests and the shooting, my behavior caught up to me and stopped me dead in my tracks.

It happened one day at school, when I was trying to protect my friend from getting jumped. This was practically a daily mission: there were many times that my friends and I would walk home or hide out at a safe haven until the bus stop was clear, just so that we wouldn't have to spend the afternoon fighting. I walked with pepper spray in the school hallways, just in case someone tried to ambush me. A few times, I even pulled the fire alarm to help save us not from fires but from fists. This was how I ultimately got kicked out of school: for practically the entire day, one of my friends had been arguing with and was being threatened by some girls from a rival gang, and she was scared she wouldn't be able to handle the fight. I snuck out of class on a hall pass and pulled the fire alarm, clearing out the entire school and giving her a chance to escape home before the girls could follow her. She escaped that ass-kicking, but I caught the wrath of the school administrators, who said they had proof that I was the one who'd pulled the fire alarm. This was the beginning of the end of my personal reign of terror at my high school; the principal had finally had enough.

It was my sister Dorothy who took me back to school a few days later. I was slumped down in the scratchy, cushioned chair next to her in the principal's office, with a devil-may-care attitude, when the administrator dropped the bomb: "She's not welcome here anymore." She justified the decision with a laundry list of offenses: every time there was an alter-cation, somehow, I was either around, in the middle of it, or had started it, and they wanted me out. "We know we have issues in this school, but she's not helping at all. I'm sorry, but she is no longer welcome here. She has to leave. Now."

Attitude or no, my heart was racing: What was I going to do? Where was I going to go? No matter how much trouble I'd caused or tried to stop, the simple fact of the matter was that I didn't think I deserved to be kicked out of school—discarded like I was some lost cause that wasn't worthy of being taught. It was embarrassing. Scary. Numbing.

"Here," the principal said coldly as she shoved a stack of papers toward my sister. "This is a list of alternative schools you might want to consider. Any number of these will be able to handle educating her in an environment that will give her the discipline she needs to get a diploma. I wish you the best of luck."

And with that, the school security guards appeared at the door to walk me to my locker—the longest walk ever. Our footsteps echoed off the cold metal framing the walls; some of those lockers I'd broken into and stole from, others I'd pushed girls into as we fought to the tooth over petty things that, really, had nothing to do with anything, especially now that I was being banished. It felt like my life was over.

When I think back on how I grew up around all that craziness and especially how it shaped my coming of age, it's hard to acknowledge that I actually thought the level of violence that pulsed through my life and that of my friends was acceptable. But we walked through the fire. Ran to it, really. I don't remember as a teenager ever saying, "I wish the violence would stop." I wasn't that progressive in my thought processes to make the leap, particularly while I was in the thick of it. But now, as an adult and a mother under my own terms, I know that the smoking, the drinking, the sex, the fighting, the gangbanging were all coping mechanisms—the means to our survival. There was real trauma there when, as children, we watched fathers disappear and mothers fight to feed, clothe, and house their families, and sisters and brothers and cousins and friends disappear into addiction and the prison system and depression or, worse, a casket. That's the kind of hand-to-hand combat we were doing on the streets of Chicago.

I can't shake the notion that these rough, sharp edges, even and especially the ones of my own making, helped shape me. Being kicked out of school in my junior year felt, at first, like death. But really, it saved my life. Immediately, it forced me out of my high school and into a military school that took charge and grew me up—made me more responsible for my actions and, certainly, more invested in my future. But the long-term benefits of growing up the way I did molded me into the perfect Marine: street-smart, ready for battle, brave enough to walk into the fire, and loyal to my allegiances. Those are strengths that have served me well in the military and in life. I wouldn't ever trade that because I know for sure that what doesn't break you makes you stronger.

You don't have to win NBA championships or hail from the streets of Chicago to be mentally tough, but having some of the following tools in your arsenal will certainly help you get past setbacks, over obstacles, and through the hardest times. Here's how you get mentally tough:

TAKE PRIDE IN WHAT YOU'RE DOING. There's an old saying: "Anything worth doing is worth doing well." Your work speaks for who you are, what value you bring to the task at hand, and really sets the tone for how others look at you, too. By extension, putting forth your very best effort strengthens your resolve and your mental fortitude, because who doesn't feel proud and accomplished when they do a job well? When I was a kid, I'd puff my chest out when I pitched in to help around the house—not because I was trying to be a brown-noser, which is what my siblings accused me of, but because I genuinely enjoyed the look on my mother's face and the warmth she would extend when I did something for her without asking. Usually, it was something as simple as bringing her something cool to drink without having to be asked. "Mom, you want some ginger ale?" I'd ask sweetly, peeking around the kitchen corner.

"That would be nice," she'd say, leaning back in the La-Z-Boy.

That small bit of happiness—hers and mine—got me through the moment and even earned me some favored treatment over my other siblings. This never went over well with them.

BE HUMBLE. As a Marine, honor, courage, and commitment are the underpinnings of every decision I make. As Tee, hard work, integrity, and passion are what I bring to all that I do. All of this and luck have taken this adopted little girl from Chicago to places I couldn't have dreamed of going, from the desert sands of Kuwait to the White House to meet the president of the United States to the set of a television show I starred in. I'm proud of my success; I earned it. But I'm always going to be Tawanda from Chicago, the woman who knows struggle—who spent much more time being a have-not than a have. I know that just as quickly as I got here, I can go back, and so I never, ever boast about what I've accomplished, where I've been, who I've met, or what I have. I choose, instead, to be humble—to keep my head down and stay grounded in the values that are important to me: appreciating my family and true friends, doing hard work, giving back to communities like those that I came from in ways that truly matter, and understanding that there is still room for improvement—still ways for me to truly stretch and grow and learn even more so I can be better and do better work in service to others. This is the way of a true warrior.

SEE THE GOOD IN YOURSELF. It was abolitionist, author, and orator Frederick Douglass who famously said, "If there is no struggle, there is no progress." In the case for building mental toughness, no truer words could be said. Mental toughness isn't just handed out in the delivery room; one has to hear the thunder, see the lightning, and weather the storm to see the rainbow—to understand that on the other side of all that you thought would ruin you is a new you: stronger, brighter, readier for life's challenges. When that happens, self-esteem blossoms, mental muscle grows, and we find that inner strength—the very core of us that can overcome what we were convinced we could not.

This was a hard concept for me to grasp when I got kicked out of school. All I could see was a long list of denials: there would be no fancy dresses, no wrist corsages, no tuxedoed prince pulling up in a fancy car to pick me up for prom. I'd never float across the huge stage in front of my family, friends, and peers and shake the principal's hand as she handed me a high school diploma. I'd never fill out a college application or trade stories about college essays and acceptance letters. My high school career was, in essence, over. The school, the administrators—all of them gave up on me. So did, it seemed, my family. I was deeply embarrassed that my behavior within the walls of my high school had such a devastating impact on my life outside of them; I felt like a failure in life, and I was only sixteen.

What was left of my future was in that stack of alternative-school brochures my sister laid out in front of my mother as she explained why I'd never darken the doorway of my old high school ever again.

"The vice principal recommended this one," Dorothy said, tapping a glossy pamphlet on the kitchen table. "It's a military school, two and a half hours away."

The look of disappointment in my mother's eyes broke my spirit—hurt more than any extension cord or house shoe ever could. I hung my head, but in a flash of incredible guilt and shame, I lifted my chin, squared my shoulders, and agreed to take my lashes.

"I know I really messed up," I said, tears rimming my eyes. "I need to make this right."

For me, the positive in going to that military school was that, upon completing the program, I'd have a diploma—and my mother's respect. I needed her to see again the good that was inside me—the kid who got good grades, was helpful around the house, and didn't bring grief to her doorstep. I knew it wouldn't be easy. But it was necessary. Believing this to my core got me mentally ready for the curriculum and tough love I would ultimately get at military school.

DO THE RIGHT THING—even and especially when it's hard to do. When you know someone is suffering and you feel deep down in your gut that he does not deserve what is happening to him, a true warrior steps in to help, not just because they don't want to see another human hurting but also because they know that helping is the right thing to do. A certain amount of mental toughness is most certainly required for this. Consider, for instance, how the needle moved in the civil rights movement after newspapers, magazines, and television stations across the country began documenting the atrocities playing out in communities across the South. The decision by Emmett Till's mother to let her son's casket remain open so that the world could witness the gruesome brutality rained on her son for allegedly whistling at the wife of a white shopkeeper required a level of mental toughness that is nearly unfathomable. But Mamie Till's choice, wrapped in that mental toughness, is regarded as a catalyst for the massive protest movement that would lead to landmark legislation untangling and eliminating federal racial segregation laws that relegated African American citizens to a modern-day caste system in the United States. Emmett's death opened the country's eyes to what was happening right up under their noses: lynchings, bombings, maimings, and many other atrocities carried out on fellow Americans just because of the color of their skin. Witnessing those cruel acts of violence then provoked compassion and sympathy from some American citizens who then, in turn, got mentally— and physically!—tough and pitched in to help change the course of history. Their sympathy and compassion had an impact, which makes them everyday warriors.

BOTTOM LINE: life can be tough, but it doesn't have to be the end of you. If you square your shoulders and use your strength as a compass, regardless of the dark, deep, painful challenges you're facing, you will find your way back to the light—to the life you want and deserve.

WARRIOR WORK

List ten ways you've been mentally tough.

_____

_____

_____

_____

_____

_____
_____
_____
_____
_____
_____
_____
_____
_____
_____
_____
_____

List ten ways you've been mentally weak. How will you become mentally tough in those areas?

_____
_____
_____
_____

_Mental toughness is spartanism with qualities of
sacrifice, self-denial, dedication. It is fearlessness,
and it is love._

—VINCE LOMBARDI, FOOTBALL COACH

3

HONOR, COURAGE, COMMITMENT: GIVE A HELPING HAND

THE WARRIOR CODE: PRINCIPLE #3

Service is the rent we pay for being. It is the very purpose of life, and not something you do in your spare time.

—MARIAN WRIGHT EDELMAN, ACTIVIST, AUTHOR

On my home office wall in a silver frame, I have a photo of Michelle Obama and me taken the evening I represented the state of Illinois at the 2012 White House "A Nation's Gratitude" dinner, hosted by President Barack Obama and the First Lady. The mission: to celebrate the more than one million Americans deployed in Operation Iraqi Freedom and Operation New Dawn and the families who supported them. It was something else to shake hands with the president and stand shoulder to shoulder with the First Lady—magical, really, because who would have ever thought Tawanda Hanible from Chicago, some two decades after being kicked out of high school, would be standing there, smiling at the first black president of the United States, in a house built by the hands of slaves, being honored for doing something good, something righteous, something altogether different from that which I'd been mixed up in as a troubled teen? The sixteen-year-old Tawanda, fresh off fighting her way through a military high school billed as her last chance to straighten up and fly right, didn't see that one coming.

The night of that White House dinner, people kept calling me a hero. But it was not a title I embraced. Still don't. I've always felt like I could be doing more, especially for kids who, like me when I was growing up in Chicago, face what seems like insurmountable odds to escape their circumstances and really win. Growing up the way I did, seeing the poverty, feeling its effects in my own house, watching it run rampant through my community, is something I will never, ever forget. That those circumstances solidified themselves and festered throughout the South Side, even after I managed to get out and change the course of my life, is, perhaps, the most disheartening of all, because I know the stakes: Chicago summers are hot and long, and when there are no resources—no camps, community programs, jobs, or anything for the people—the people find trouble. Particularly the kids. Over and over while I worked as a Marine recruiter, I kept coming across kids who, because they didn't qualify to join the corps, ended up going back to the same communities—and destructive ways—they were trying to escape. It is a vicious cycle.

I am a product of that cycle, but I got the helping hand I needed to turn my life around. I received it two and a half hours south of Chicago, in Rantoul, Illinois, where Lincoln's Challenge Academy was based. Lincoln's Challenge is a youth intervention program that uses a military model to whip at-risk kids into shape. It is a last-chance school—a place where students are put through military paces to gather the education, coping skills, discipline, and structure they need to detour them off the road to incarceration, gang violence, drugs, and any other vice that threatens to end their young lives. I have to be honest: it was hard to accept that I was one of those kids who needed this type of intervention, but if it would make things right with my family and save face for my being kicked out of school, I was down to go. I messed up; this was my way of fixing it.

Still, the ride to Lincoln's Challenge was a long one; I was filled with regret and trepidation—regret because my actions got me kicked out of school and trepidation because I was about to be dropped off, yet again, on the doorstep of strangers and expected to make it a home for the next six months. By the time we arrived, I'd put my game face on—hardened myself, ready to walk the gauntlet of judgmental, prying eyes wondering about the new kid on campus. They were sizing me up, but I was doing some mental judgments of my own.

This much I know: Lincoln's Challenge was not playing with us kids. This was no dumping ground for wayward students until we "aged out" of traditional public school or whatever system we were in; the school, a quasi-military academy located on an old military base and run by active National Guard members and instructors who'd served in the armed services, was legitimately designed and meant to break us down and build us back up into the kinds of humans who could ditch our ugly ways and go on to become productive members of society. I didn't realize it as I was going through it, but I came to understand that what the school demanded of us was as close to being in the military as one could get without actually being in the armed forces. It was exactly like the boot camp I went through to become a Marine, except the recruits were kids. There was absolutely no room for individuality: we wore identical uniforms to classes, to work, and even to bed; we all woke up at 5:30 A.M., exercised together, ate together, showered together, studied together, performed community service together, did laundry together, and turned out the lights together, all on the same schedule, every day of the week. There was a lot of "yes, ma'ams" and "no, ma'ams" and standing at attention and running in formation and standing with our faces toward a wall for the simplest of offenses. Our days were so structured there was no time to be upset about it. Seriously. There literally was not time for it.

Running and exercising weren't a problem for me; hell, I'd already had much practice with that on the streets of Chicago. But those 5:30 A.M. wake-up calls were threatening to be the death of me. My first day rising that early didn't go over too well; my lackadaisical attitude, coupled with my excessive eye rolling, only helped launch me to the top of the instructor's shit list.

Still, I started out walking the straight and narrow: going to classes, being where I was supposed to be when I was supposed to be there, doing my homework, keeping to myself—basically doing my time so I could get my GED and get out of there. But my desire to do right sometimes became overshadowed by my bad attitude, which could rear its ugly head at the slightest provocation. If someone said something to me sideways, I was quick to run my mouth—would curse out fellow cadets, instructors, anybody who thought they could tell me how to be.

This, of course, kept me in all kinds of trouble; I got punished for talking crazy and being rude and disobedient.

The one who caught the brunt of my ire was this one particular girl, Shanay. Eventually, she and I became the best of friends, and to this day, we keep in touch, but way before we got to the solid relationship we have now, we hated each other—enough to try to kill. Well, at least do as much damage to one another as we possibly could. I hated her, for starters, because she belonged to a rival gang and got kicked out of the rival high school back home in Chicago. She repped her set, while I made sure to always rep the 9. It was in the cards for us to be enemies. A relationship forged out of mutual circumstances should have been what we had from the beginning. Instead, we had been groomed to hate each other strictly because this was the code of the streets. I often made sure to show off my right ear of six piercings, signifying my allegiance to where I was from, which, of course, would oftentimes instigate an argument. This was my way of making sure she knew I wasn't anybody's pushover.

But really, we were one and the same person. She was a survivor, having practically raised herself and her siblings in a single-parent home while her own mother battled her addictions, leaving Shanay in charge. She was self-sufficient and tough-talking, as was I. And we both wanted to be in charge, which meant that whenever it was time for us to accomplish anything together, there would be fighting and bloodshed, with whatever room our altercation took place in destroyed. No area was safe when we bumped heads.

I guess I can admit that it was I who kicked off our ugliest fight. She asked for it. I mean, here we were, a bunch of badasses in an alternative school for a myriad of infractions and she was careless enough to sleep on securing her locker. She just left it open for anybody to rifle through. So I did what any self-respecting rival would do: I took all her stuff out and tossed it into the garbage. Not just any ol' garbage, mind you: I dragged the garbage can from the bathroom out to the hall where the lockers were and tossed her things on top of dirty sanitary napkins, balls of hair, snotty tissues, and anything else gross one would find in a garbage can that lives in a room where people groom themselves and clean up natural bodily functions.

To retaliate, she took everything of mine she could get her hands on, dumped it in the shower, and turned on the water. I responded with my hands. To be honest, I wasn't upset about my personal items as much as I was intent on never showing weakness. Looking back on it, I guess we were the original Bad Girls Club.

It was just a matter of time before our retaliatory behavior came to a head, and that head popped one particular afternoon in the laundry room. This time, I'd dumped all those nasty contents from the bathroom garbage can onto her bed. It just felt like the right thing to do at that moment, particularly after she said something disrespectful enough to get a rise out of me. Words were exchanged, and before we knew it, we were cursing, then pushing, then slapping, then punching, then embroiled in a full-out war, our bodies spilling over furniture and fellow students and the floor and walls. Heart racing, rage pulsing, breath heavy, I leaped over a bench with every intention of body slamming her and landing with my hands around her neck, but I fell short. Instead, a jagged piece of metal jutting out from that bench sliced through my leg; I felt a pain as searing as a serrated knife slicing through my calf. Blood was everywhere. And by the time the adults found their way into the laundry room and pulled us apart, we were both bloody, battle-scarred, and full of a rage that made us practically unrecognizable.

We got sent to what was the equivalent of the principal's office, where administrators were charged with deciding our fate. This had become almost a standard practice for us: we'd fight, someone would break it up, we'd end up in the office, we'd get punished. But this time, they aimed to teach us a lesson—to make it so that we would put an end to all the fighting.

"Tomorrow at sundown, the two of you are going outside on the course," the head of the disciplinary board said as Shanay and I stood at attention. I could practically taste the anger in the spittle she was spraying in my face. "Since the two of you think you're so tough, let's see how you do out there, with nothing to depend on but each other."

Understand, this was the ultimate punishment: to be sent out to the obstacle course, where we'd have to prove our strength, agility, and endurance on a boot camp–style series of exercises that would make grown men cry for mercy. I'd heard about it from several cadets who'd made it through and witnessed up close what happened when others couldn't finish the challenge; those who gave up packed up and went home—marked as failures who didn't have the discipline, strength, or dogged determination to make something better of themselves. Being sent to the course was, really, the last stop before one became a high school dropout.

I didn't know—or care about—what Shanay wanted, but I

did know this: I couldn't be the one in my family who didn't have a high school diploma or GED. Being that kind of failure wasn't an option for me. Giving up was not my portion. I would go to the course determined, ready to do what was necessary to stay and finish my mission.

I was scared, though. I spent the entire day with my stomach in knots, my mind racing, dreading sundown, knowing that I'd be pushed to my very limit. The hours leading up to the challenge were meant to be used to get mentally and physically ready for what was to come.

"Drink lots of water," a few of my fellow cadets warned. "You don't want to get dehydrated out there."

"They gonna be in your face, screaming on you," another added. "Just focus on what you gotta do."

The walk to the obstacle course might as well have been a death march, that's how scary and intimidating it was. In the dead of night, it was hard to see so much as my hand in front of my own face, let alone the obstacle course meant to break me down. All the yelling the instructors were doing in my face made it that much more terrifying. I looked nervously at Shanay, who looked equally petrified.

"On your mark!" an instructor yelled as we stood at the line, ready to run. "Go!"

Shanay and I took off running and, for hours, climbed walls, crawled under barbed wire, ran through tires and mud, rolled logs, jumped hurdles, climbed ropes, ran—you name it, we did it. There was no cooldown time, no water breaks— just us and the instructors at our backs, hurling screams intended to break us down to our absolute lowest point so that the only thing we could do was submit to being built back up again. I did my best to tune them out, instead focusing on the voice in my head: *Just get through it, Tee. At the end of this is a shower and your bed. You can do it. You're strong. You're here for a purpose. And you cannot be the only child to get kicked out of high school and never graduate. Suck it up and do whatever you need to do to get through this.*

I made it. So did Shanay. I wish I could tell you that we learned our lesson—that our time that night on the course was the first and last time we walked through the fire. It wasn't. Shanay and I would find ourselves out there a second time after yet another knockdown, drag-out fight over God knows what, this go-round even more brutal than the first.

Shanay was so overwhelmed that she tearily surrendered. "I don't want to do this anymore!" she yelled. "I want to go home!"

That was a turning point for her and for me.

"Come on, Shanay," I said, rushing over to help her up out the dirt, where she'd collapsed into a heap of hysterics. "You got this," I added, telling her something, anything, to keep her moving. We finished that course, both of us in tears, side by side, together.

I'd find myself on that course one more time after that, this time by myself. For the life of me, I can't really explain why, back then, I chose to do everything the hard way. It's not rocket science to understand that if I'd just kept my head down, done my work, and checked my attitude and mouth, I could have done my time, graduated, gotten my GED, and gone back home and started over again. But consequences meant nothing to me in the heat of the moment; whether I was in a verbal argument or a physical brawl, everything would literally become a blur and I'd have a sole goal: to fight to win.

Eventually, though, I fell in line. Somewhere along the way, while having the school's core objectives drilled into my skull—while stressing academic excellence, leadership, job readiness, and physical fitness, the school also drilled into us the virtues of responsible citizenship, service to the community, health, sex education and nutrition, and life-coping skills—I focused on acing my classes and the practice GED tests, tutoring fellow students, and doing community service to earn my biweekly stipend, which got me the money I needed to buy my toiletries and even a few extras during Sunday trips to big-box stores like Walmart and Target.

Those six months at Lincoln's Challenge were, without a doubt, some of the loneliest months of my life. There were no breaks—no time that I could go back to Chicago to have dinner with my family or hang out on the stoop with my friends. Visitations from family members were allowed on Sundays, but I never saw my family—no one came to see me. My mother didn't have a car and she was elderly, and my older sisters, Dorothy and Patricia, were too busy with their own lives to bring our mom on the more-than-two-hour journey to see me, so I'd just mentally check out while everyone else around me visited with their families. Though there was one guy who caught my eye, I didn't even mess around with boys. Eventually, I gave up my belligerence and focused on the end goal: graduation.

Even that was a sad little affair for me. Though graduation was set up as a celebration at the academy, replete with a ceremony and certificates and all the pomp and circumstance reserved for such a monumental occasion, I went through it alone. No one from my family came to celebrate with me. At the end of it all, I packed up my things, tucked my certificate into my bag, and went back to Chicago, having graduated a full year ahead of my peers, feeling accomplished and ready for the world—and primed for a life in the military. The latter, I just didn't know yet.

What I did know then, though, as I do now, is that Lincoln's Challenge saved my life.

I caught quite a few lucky breaks as a kid, trouble notwithstanding. Though abandoned by my birth mother, I was adopted by a family that loved and cared for me. Though I was kicked out of high school, I was taken in by a military school that not only gave me a second chance to earn a diploma and stay out of jail but also pointed me in the direction of the armed services. I was a young adult full of attitude, with a predilection for street gangs and alcohol, but my sister saw enough potential in me to get me down to the recruiting office and make me see that I had what it took to become a Marine. And the Marines trusted my strength, intelligence, and abilities enough to allow me two decades of dedicated service to the toughest, most faithful organization this side of the moon. Oorah!

So who would I be to take in all that goodwill and fortune and refuse to do the same for someone else's child? Embracing my own journey and getting an up-close look at the lives of others made me more understanding—made me try to hold on to the good in us. The God in us. I've always felt it my duty to give back in some way—to help the community of children who are facing off against the same challenges I did as a kid, and to return the favor extended to me by all the angels who kept me lifted along my turbulent teen years. These were ordinary people who did extraordinary things to help a kid like me stay alive and make it out. They are super-heroes. They are warriors.

This was what I focused on when I became a recruiter in my own right. It wasn't an easy proposition: I had to try to convince black families, already suspect of the government and leery of sending their children off to serve with the real possibility that they could end up fighting in a war, that it was okay for their sons and daughters to join the Marine Corps. My pitch—that the Marine Corps is full of jobs that don't necessarily translate into a Marine going off to war—would fall on deaf ears. Sometimes, it would get violent, like the time I talked one young man through the entire process—I gave him the hard sell on what he could do for his country and what the Marine Corps could do for him, and he even took the practice test—and went to his mother's house to get her to sign the parental consent. Fresh from work and not in the mood, she came to the living room where I was standing with a pair of scissors raised high in the air. "Get the hell out of my house!" she demanded. "He's not going anywhere with you!"

Needless to say, I didn't get anything done that night. When someone pulls out scissors and orders you to get gone, you get the hell out of the house, no matter what military uniform you're wearing. Eventually, I won her over, though; I took her and her son, Chris, out to dinner, and we talked about our shared experiences and familial political views before she finally agreed to let her son join the reserves, the only option that made her even remotely comfortable. Later, when he was old enough to make the decision on his own, he went into active duty, but we had to work through it every step of the way. I was willing to put in that work because the kids I was recruiting in the North Carolina neighborhoods I was covering reminded me of me. For some recruiters, they were just bodies—a quota to fill. But to me, they were kids who needed a chance, a break—something to be a part of so that they could get out of the streets and just . . . live.

I ended up being a huge success because of my personal connection and gentle touch; I always included the families in the decision-making and sold them on the Marine Corps with the same zeal that I did the kids. I would make the connection even more visceral by explaining to them that I was a mom with two daughters who traveled and enjoyed my job, but who could have just as easily stayed in the streets after having been kicked out of high school and wandered a bit, completely missing the opportunities that I ultimately reaped by joining the Marine Corps. This allowed the families to see me as human—as someone who genuinely cared about seeing the kids in our community win.

I led with my heart.

Sometimes, I would extend that authenticity and helping hand to kids who weren't Marine Corps material. One teen, Brandon, was a whip-smart kid, but he ran with the wrong crowd, and I knew that it was just a matter of time before he made a bad decision or got caught up around someone else who did. To keep him out of trouble, I made him an assistant in my office; he'd do cold calls, run errands, use my car to pick other teens I had working in my office up from school. I'd plan trips to the movies and bowling, and we'd come in like a mob, having the best time. This allowed them to see the good side of the Marine Corps—a part that they wouldn't see until after a year of training, but a sight they needed to see nonetheless, to be sure that we Marines weren't a bunch of boogeymen looking to steal them into the night. Truly, there's nothing like seeing older Marines share life stories with teens who deserve the energy and mentoring, and have them actually have fun competing and bonding and exchanging that good energy with one another.

Indeed, this was the impetus for my starting Operation Heroes Connect. In 2011, I took my efforts to help children out of the recruitment offices and directly into the streets: with the help of my friend Nancy, I founded Operation Heroes Connect, a nonprofit organization that matches returning military veterans and kids who come from rough backgrounds. It's a connection that makes incredible sense: veterans are returning home from service in search of opportunities that give a chance to participate in something bigger than themselves, much like what they've experienced in the military; the kids are looking for mentors to support, listen to, and guide them. Score! We go directly into challenging places like homeless shelters and pair kids between ages seven and seventeen with veterans who offer role modeling, friendship, assistance, and the attentive ear the kids need to change the trajectory of their lives. When we're not facilitating those partnerships, we're in the community, donating our time and resources to homeless shelters, organizing food drives, and finding other ways to be a blessing to the communities that need our help.

What transpires is more heroic than anything I could have ever accomplished in the desert sands of Kuwait: these kids find their way out of the darkness, and the veterans who help them find a sense of purpose after they come home and are anxious to do something constructive. Ultimately, they become heroes for each other. Of this, I'm proudest of all.

BEING IN SERVICE TO OTHERS IS A HALLMARK of being a warrior. It helps us develop and grow, puts our expertise to good use, and even develops new skills as we dedicate our time to taking on interesting, challenging opportunities. Volunteering is pure: you're not getting paid, you're giving someone a helping hand; you're not taking anything from anyone, you're giving yourself, your time, your skill; you're not counting on anyone paying you back, you're contributing in immeasurable ways that, to a person in need, are absolutely priceless. Volunteering is also incredibly rewarding: what feels better than standing back, checking out your handiwork, and seeing the transformation you helped put in motion? It's the closest thing to feeling like you've put on a cape and become an everyday superhero.

Not sure where to start or how to pitch in for the greater good? Try the following:

TWENTY-FIVE WAYS WARRIORS GIVE BACK

1. Mentor a child.

2. Read to, sing with, play games with, or simply talk to elders at a retirement home.

3. Shelve books or host story time readings at your local library.

4. Are you good at math or writing? Tutor at your local school.

5. Habitat for Humanity is always looking for someone who can swing a hammer, paint a wall, or install a window.

6. Get all hands on deck with Purple Heart Homes, which is always on the lookout for help building, maintaining, painting, landscaping, decorating, or making handicapped-accessible homes for veterans returning from service.

7. Help collect food or raise funds for the local food pantry.

8. Be a dog walker for a local animal rescue shelter, or offer your home as a foster care for cats waiting to be adopted.

9. National parks always need extra hands on deck to clean up litter, lead tours, and help with beautification.

10. Play an instrument? Volunteer for Musicians On Call, an organization that delivers live, in-room performances to hospital patients who are undergoing procedures or are confined to their beds.

11. They may not wear the candy stripe getups anymore, but hospital volunteers are still extremely appreciated when they help visitors navigate the facilities or deliver reading material to patients.

12. The Red Cross doesn't just look for volunteer blood donors; the organization is always in the market for people who can do everything from helping displaced families to comforting injured service members or veterans to instructing teens how to be babysitters.

13. Pitch in with KaBOOM!, an organization whose volunteers improve and build playgrounds in challenged communities where children have little green space to play.

14. Throw a birthday party—complete with a cake and presents—for children and families living in homeless shelters, who all too often miss out on special celebrations because of their unstable living situations.

15. Send a card or care package to a soldier who doesn't get much by way of regular mail or packages through Any Soldier, an organization that connects donors to military units with soldiers who could use a little personal and emotional lift.

16. Up your peace of mind, get to know your neighbors, and get good food to the people who need it most by planting, picking, and harvesting produce at a community garden that donates food to local food banks.

17. Forget getting presents for your birthday or Christmas. Instead, direct gift-givers to donate to a charity you love.

18. Be a good neighbor: check in on single moms and seniors living alone in your neighborhood; maybe they need help with a home repair, or babysitting, or just a grown-up conversation with a kind person.

19. Calling aestheticians, makeup artists, and nail techs: the public service program Look Good Feel Better pairs beauty professionals with people with cancer to help them manage appearance-related side effects of cancer treatment, including lessons on skin and nail care, makeup application, wigs and turbans, accessories, and styling.

20. Open a pet food pantry that serves families in need who have pets.

21. Drive elderly or sick neighbors to their medical appointments, to the grocery store, or to see friends they can't otherwise see without transportation.

22. Mentor or tutor a child in foster care, or pitch in with Foster Care to Success, a nonprofit organization that needs volunteers to help college-bound foster care students prepare for higher education.

23. Host a drive for formalwear—dresses and tuxedos—and donate the clothing to low-income high school students who want to go to prom but can't afford formal outfits.

24. Give a teacher a break: pick a favorite children's picture book and volunteer to be a guest reader in a local elementary school.

25. Commit a small act of kindness: pay for the coffee of the person behind you at the coffee shop, help a fellow shopper load her groceries into the car, or tell a lady she looks beautiful today.

The truth of the matter is it doesn't take much by way of experience or super special skills to be helpful—to change something as little as someone's day or something as big as someone's life. Our society needs us to be those everyday heroes willing to help those in need.

WARRIOR WORK

In what ways have you been an everyday hero to someone else?

_____

_____

_____

_____

_____

_____

_____

_____

_____

_____

_____

List the skills you possess that can be put to good use in service of others.

_____

_____

_____

_____

_____

_____

_____

_____

_____

_____

_____

_____

List the names and contact information for organizations to which you can lend your skills in the service of others.

_____

_____

_____

_____

_____

_____

_____

_____

_____

_____

_____

_____

_____

_____

_____

The best way to find yourself is to lose yourself in the service of others.

—MAHATMA GANDHI

4

SEMPER FLEXIBILUS (ALWAYS FLEXIBLE): GET OUT OF YOUR OWN WAY

THE WARRIOR CODE: PRINCIPLE #4

I am the greatest obstacle to my greatest dreams.

—*CRAIG D. LOUNSBROUGH, LICENSED PROFESSIONAL
COUNSELOR, AUTHOR*

Getting in your own way" is a simple concept that has serious consequences: it's when we let anxiety, self-doubt, ego, and/or pressure stand between our ambitions and ourselves. Unfortunately, all too many of us are content to climb aboard that train; we set goals for ourselves or vow to stop bad habits and break negative cycles, only to allow our best-laid plans to be derailed. Oftentimes, we're the conductors who drove the train right off the tracks. We swear we'll quit smoking cigarettes, or stop running up the balance on our credit cards, or dust off that old business plan and get back to jump-starting that entrepreneurial adventure we always wanted to pursue, and then we'll sabotage it all. Out of fear of failure. Out of laziness. Because it's more comfortable to be stuck than it is to do the work it takes to climb out of the muck. Sometimes it's a little of all three. When we derail, we have no one to blame but ourselves.

I know this was the case for me. I wish I could tell you that my stint in military school changed me—got me away from the gangs and the weed and alcohol and the trouble and put me on the road to redemption. I mean, I did have a GED in hand and a little "get right" in me after going through six months of learning and living under the strict, disciplined leadership of armed services vets. I felt incredibly accomplished when I went back home and my friends were still working their way through school and trying hard to get what I already had: a diploma.

But the truth of the matter was that though I had changed, Chicago had not—at least not my little sliver of the South Side. And with not much to do but sit around the house alone—by then, my brother had joined the Marines, my sister Nichole was in college, and I was the last kid standing, stuck in the house with my elderly mother—trouble was waiting just down the street, around practically every corner. It was easy, so very easy, for me to fall right back into my old ways with my old friends who were walking down the same streets, hanging with the same crews, doing all the same things they'd been doing before I left—the very things that got me in trouble in the first place. The pull was much too strong for me to overcome; before I knew it, I was back on the streets, strolling the 9, drinking and smoking weed and sinking back into the destructive ways that, before my time at Lincoln's Challenge, seemed to always keep me on the edge of personal destruction.

And then came the afternoon that I almost died.

It seemed, at the time, like a great idea: seven of us piled into a car, with the windows rolled up, smoking weed, with the glint of the hot Chicago summer sun bouncing off the glass. I was there for this boy I liked. He invited me, and who was I to turn down the opportunity to sit next to him, joking, laughing, and just enjoying each other's company?

"It's hot in here," I said after a while. "Can we crack the window just a little bit?"

"Nah," one of my friends said as he puffed. "The contact is better with them up."

What he said made sense, I guess, but really, how good could my judgment have been considering I'd been smoking weed in a crowded, hot car? All I remember is thinking, *I need to get out of here*. My body was starting to rebel against the entire situation: I could actually hear my own heart racing, even over the loud music thumping from the speakers, and I could feel my skin overheating and getting clammy. Before I knew it, I was hallucinating and hearing voices telling me to get out of the car. I obeyed the call.

"I'm going to go outside for a bit," I said, reaching over the guy I was sitting next to and grabbing the handle of the car door. I crawled over him and stumbled out of the ride onto the hard concrete; the air was pulsing with heat, making it hard for me to breathe. I clawed at my shirt as I stumbled to the front lawn of a nearby house and, in what felt like slow-motion, fell to my knees and stretched out on the grass like I was lying down for a good night's rest. "Oh my God, this grass feels so cold and so cool on my skin," I slurred.

And then everything—the sky, the grass, the car, my friends, the lady who rushed over to me from the front door of the house where I was lying to ask me if I was all right—all of it blinked to black.

I woke up on a gurney in the emergency room, a bunch

of IVs and beeping machines snaking from my arms, and my sister Dorothy standing over me, her head in her hand, teary. "Hey," I croaked, my mouth and throat desert dry from having tubes shoved down them. "Where am I?"

"South Shore Hospital," Dorothy said, rubbing my hand. "You gave us a scare."

"Why am I here? What happened?" I asked, attempting to sit up.

"No, no, you have to keep still," Dorothy said, gently pushing me back down on the bed. "You're going to be here for a little while."

My sister went on to explain that the doctors thought I'd overheated from sitting in the hot car but that they were going to keep me for observation to make sure that nothing else was wrong.

"They said you were smoking marijuana," she added. She didn't say she was disappointed, but I could tell by her voice— by the way her eyes pierced through me—that she was fed up with my mess.

To this day, I don't know if Dorothy told our mother the truth of what happened that day; I convinced myself that my mother simply thought the Chicago heat, which reached above one hundred and five degrees that day, got the best of me. What I do know is that after that incident, my mother sat me down for "the talk," a frank, one-way conversation about the need for me to get up, get out, and do something beyond sleeping through the morning, hanging out all hours of the day and night with my friends, and depending on her to give me a little change here and there to go out. The Job Corps was mentioned. So were the wanted ads. All I could hear, really, was a threat: if I didn't get my act together, I'd be sent away. There I was, seventeen years old and firm in my roots with my mother and adoptive family, but still, the trauma of thinking my behavior could have me sent away from the only home I'd known still haunted me. I didn't want any trouble; I just wanted to be left alone to hang out with whom I wanted, when I wanted, without being stuck in the house up under my mother, who, at her age, simply couldn't understand the call of the streets.

To keep her off my back, I went and found myself a job at a local fast-food chain, Italian Fiesta, a pizza joint known for its thin-crust pizza. I lasted all of three days.

Day one, I was trained to take orders from both walk-ins and those who called in to the restaurant, plus work the register. I made it through the whole shift, but I was bored out of my mind; all I could think about was the fun I was missing out on that evening at the beach, where all my friends had gone to party. Day two, I left the house at the same time as if I were heading to my shift, but instead I hopped on the bus to hang out with my girl Shanay, the girl who was my archenemy at Lincoln's Challenge but who ultimately became a good friend. She now lived in an area of Chicago called Jeffery Manor, and because that was one of my stomping grounds—my cousins lived there, too—I had no concern with being on the wrong side of the tracks. I knew that she and I would do something a lot more fun than passing out pizza. I didn't even bother to call my manager to say I wasn't coming in; I just got dressed, said goodbye to my mother, headed to Shanay's, and did exactly the opposite of what I'd promised my mother I would do: I blew off any and all responsibility and sank deeper into the muck with my friends.

On day three, I thought, *Hey, maybe I should get back to work.* And, as if it was an option to just work when I felt like it, I climbed into my uniform, put a big smile on my face, and walked into Italian Fiesta with a renewed sense of motivation, trying my best to look both cheery and contrite as I went to the back room to punch in. The manager looked me up and down and smirked.

"Oh, you don't work here anymore," he said, shaking his head.

"But I—"

"You're fired."

There was no talking him out of firing me, and I knew I deserved what he dished out. But I wasn't nearly as disappointed about being fired as I was scared to tell my mother I'd lost my job. In fact, I actually skipped telling her I'd gotten fired and instead hit the pavement looking for a new gig, fully intending on doing right by this one so that I wouldn't have to worry about explaining away the Italian Fiesta incident.

Alas, a new job wasn't in the cards; chalk it up to youthful inexperience and a smidge of thickheadedness, but I had no idea how hard it would be to find work in our neighborhood, where unemployment rates were consistently higher for black residents. Nobody was hiring. And I was scared—scared of not being able to earn my keep and especially scared of the consequences my mother would mete out after finding out I was fired for choosing my friends over my responsibilities.

Mom was hot. "So what are you going to do with your

life?" she demanded, struggling to sit up in the oversize La-Z-Boy recliner she favored when she watched television.

Ten years earlier, her words would have been punctuated by some choice licks with the weapon of her choice. But I was too old to beat, and she was too old by then to beat me. She would have to lean on something altogether different to inspire me to get my act together: I would have to own up to my mistakes and get laser-sharp focused on accountability and responsibility, because that's what adults do.

"You need to think seriously about what you're going to do with the rest of your life, because what you're doing now is not working. Not for you, not for me, not for anybody."

Then, instead of letting me ponder a few ideas of my own, my mother decided for me: I would go into the military. "Your brother is in the Marines, and he's doing just fine there. I think you need to get on down to that recruiting office and see about joining."

I HAD EVERY INTENTION of looking into what I'd need to do to join either the navy or air force, but Dorothy pushed me into it a little sooner than I'd planned. She invited me to go shopping with her, and I happily rode shotgun, only to end up at a local recruiting office.

"Really?" I said, annoyed when I realized where we were.

"Really," Dorothy said, resolute. "Let's go. You're going to talk to these people today. Right now."

Slowly, I climbed out of the car and dragged myself through the front door of the small, neat recruiting office.

I didn't know much about the military, but I was sure joining the Marines wasn't for me. I loved that it had changed my brother's life—he joined when he was seventeen, and his decision got him out of Chicago, afforded him the opportunity to travel the world, and even set him up to meet and marry his wife and have a beautiful little baby—but I actually knew nothing about the Marines as an institution. I honestly had never even seen females in the Marine Corps commercials. I didn't want any parts of that, so I made a beeline straight for the desk of the navy recruiter. Thing is, whoever was supposed to be manning it was out to lunch. The same went for the air force and army recruiters: no one was there.

I slowly turned toward the desk of the Marine recruiter, and there he was, smiling and waving and beckoning me over to his corner of the room. I knew the guy: Staff Sergeant Guzman was the same man who'd recruited my brother. It was he who'd sat in my parents' living room, stating the case for why they should give my brother parental consent to join the Marines before he was of age, and he, too, who'd secured permission for my brother to leave boot camp to attend our adopted father's funeral. I remember staring at him as he stood by my brother's side at the grave site, shoulders squared, head up, staring straight ahead, his uniform crisp and perfect. He was impressive, even to this then fifteen-year-old hardheaded girl who'd already begun a slow, destructive walk down the wrong path.

I remember Dorothy asking most of the questions: she wanted to know how soon I could leave, if I could pick where I wanted to be based, how much I'd get paid and how often. Hell, you would've thought the roles were reversed and she was the one going to boot camp.

What was supposed to be a quick visit would end up turning into a multihour meeting. Before I could get in a word edgewise, he was dusting off a chair and desk for me to sit down and take a practice entry test to see if I even qualified.

"Now, you seem like a smart young lady," he said, "but getting into the Marines won't be easy for you, especially because you're female. The scoring is different because they need to make sure you can hold your own with the best of the best. The guys can score thirty-five. Girls need at least a fifty to get in. You think you can handle that?"

I looked at the practice test he set in front of me and nodded. It didn't occur to me to question why the scoring inequity existed; my seventeen-year-old self was much too young to recognize just how much the rules were tipped against women, even as early as the enlistment process.

About an hour later, after taking the test, I sat down at the recruiter's desk as he laid a bunch of colored rectangular cards in front of me, each of them listing all the things the Marines could do for me. By the time he finished, I was strolling out of the recruitment office with a smile on my face, excited. I'd scored high enough on the practice test for the recruiter to schedule me for the real thing, signaling that I had what it took to make it in the branch that, earlier, I'd quietly sworn I wanted no part of. My mother saw the light in my face when I marched through the front door, and she listened intently while I told her excitedly that, finally, I had a plan for my life.

"I'm going to travel the world and see all these different countries and help out in all these different places," I said, words tumbling out of my mouth. That's what sold me: not the idea of getting money for an education or defending my country but knowing that going into the Marines would get me out of Chicago. There I was, seventeen years old, and I had left my city only once in my life, to go to a wedding in Ohio—and we'd driven there. I'd never seen the inside of an airplane, much less traveled on one. Going into the Marines, leaving all I'd ever known, a lot of it not good for me—the gangs, the drugs and alcohol, the men I'd been messing around with, my personal self-destruction. That few hours with the recruiter shone a light on a path I hadn't seen.

I couldn't wait to tell my brother I was planning on joining him in the Marines. He gave me all of about two sentences before he torpedoed my hopes and dreams.

"You're not going to make it in the Marine Corps," he said just as easily as one says, "Pass the salt."

I got really quiet.

"This is not for you," he continued. "You need to go back and talk to the air force recruiter."

Now understand, it broke my heart to have my brother say, without hesitation, that I wasn't cut out to be a Marine—to be like him. I looked up to my big brother, sure, but when he went into the service, he morphed into my hero. After all, he'd seen his entire life change in the military: he'd made it out of Chicago, and his success at his job had translated to success in life. When I'd seen him just the Thanksgiving before, he showed up to the dinner table with a new baby, my niece, who was the product of a loving marriage. I was so proud of him, enjoying his meal, surrounded by a family—a family he'd created. My brother had made it.

But here he was, telling me that I didn't have what it took

to accomplish what he had. By the time I was ready to hang up the phone with him, I decided my brother was probably right: I should hitch a ride back to the recruiting station and talk to the air force guy. It took me all of about sixty seconds to morph from "My brother's got a point" to "Screw my brother: I *am* good enough; I *can* do this."

I got angry.

Then I got focused.

It would be easy to chalk up my irrational behavior—choosing to sink back into my old ways, hanging with the same destructive crowd, doing the same destructive things, working overtime to lose a good job—to youth. This, after all, is what we do for kids who mess up continuously and refuse to get their acts together: we extend them grace by blaming their setbacks and failures on youthful indiscretion, immaturity, a bit of thickheadedness, and, in some cases, a lack of opportunities.

But when I take stock of how I was conducting myself back then, I have to put some of that blame squarely on my own shoulders. Having come back from military school with a GED and six months of military training, discipline, and "get right" under my belt, there was no reason for me to head back into the streets, knowing what I'd find there—knowing what would find me. Really, I wasn't too young to recognize that.

But it was easier to fall back into those old habits—hanging with the old crew, smoking and drinking, falling for the guy who showed me not much more than a little interest—than it was to do what my mother had demanded of me and what

I should have been ready to do for myself: do something constructive with my life. I didn't realize it back then, but as an adult, I know this much to be true: I was much more content getting in my own way.

It is possible to get out of your own way. But it requires you to do the labor—to let go of your anxiety, recognize your potential, remove the obstacles you've set up for yourself, and put yourself on a strict regimen of accountability. Here's how:

STOP BEING A BAG LADY. We all have something that's hurt us—something that contributes to who we are. But some of us act as if we are the sum of all our pain; we let that baggage weigh down our ability to live fully and out loud. Erykah Badu spoke truth into this very subject in her song "Bag Lady": "Pack light," she sang. Acknowledge the things that hurt you in the past—that kicked your ass—but don't let them weigh down your ability to get bigger. Letting them define you is a heavy load to bear, and it stops your ability to move on dead in its tracks. I know now, for instance, that my being involved with the gangs was about much more than hanging out and having fun; I was seeking that deep familial connection that I thought I'd been missing when my birth father died and my birth mother abandoned my brother and me, and dulling the pain of that particular hurt with destructive behavior, like smoking marijuana, drinking alcohol, and having sex without anything more than a surface relationship and half-hearted commitment. I had to actively choose to put that baggage down and run toward something that would give me purpose and meaning—that would lift me instead of hampering my journey. Making the conscious decision to let go of the baggage helps us free ourselves from the past that binds us and run toward the more important work of living the life we truly want.

BE CLEAR ABOUT WHAT YOU WANT and commit to it. The very first step around that huge roadblock you've set up for yourself? Being really clear about what your goal is. Be intentional—declare it. "In two months' time, I will no longer be a smoker." "I will cut down my debt by half by year's end." "I'm going to go back to college to earn my master's so that I can get that job of my dreams." Write it down in a journal, or, even better, pop it on a sticky note or two and hang them around your house where you have to see and acknowledge it: the bathroom mirror, the refrigerator, your nightstand. Setting the goal and committing to a specific time frame is the strongest first step you can take toward your goal because you've set the intention, with the understanding that there will be a reward at the end of your journey—a reward that will help make you so much happier than sitting around feeling sorry about your lot in life.

ELIMINATE THE DISTRACTIONS. Anything—or anyone—who throws you off your game has got to go. In my case, it was the lure of partying with my friends that drew me away from handling my responsibility to my job and, ultimately, my mother, who simply wanted me to get focused on the next phase of my life: adulthood. Maybe your distraction is that coworker who always invites you to join him for that afternoon smoke break, or that one friend who always invites you out to fancy restaurants where you end up spending way too much money on dinner and cocktails. How are you going to quit smoking or erase that debt if you're consistently saying yes to the people and situations that consistently throw you off your game? You can't get to what you truly want until you agree to change the habits and the people and situations that encourage them.

BE MINDFUL OF WHAT YOU'RE CRAVING. Face it: sometimes what you're trying to stay away from can't be avoided. The people closest to you—the ones you can't toss to the curb, like a spouse, child, or roommate—can sabotage your best efforts by partaking in the very thing you're trying to kick. For instance, it would be great to have your husband join you on your journey to eliminating alcohol from your diet, but you can't stop him from enjoying a glass of wine with dinner if he hasn't joined you in the commitment to stop drinking. Similarly, you can't tell the grocery store to stop frying chicken because the smell of it makes you want to kick that new vegan diet to the curb. When this happens, don't run away: get mindful. Smelling that food or wine is a trigger, sure, but you've got to get used to kicking that willpower into high gear, and the only way you'll be able to do that is to let the cravings hit you and then get gone. You don't have to engage them. You don't have to avoid them. Smell the food. Watch your man drink the wine. Keep running past that park bench you desperately want to sit on rather than jog. You won't combust. You'll just be getting out of your own way and moving on to a more mindful way of doing the new you— the new you that can't be controlled by a smell or someone else's actions.

FLAT-HAND NAYSAYERS. Really, what they have to say about your commitment to get out of your own way and run through the wall to get to the better version of you is inconsequential, especially if their words are discouraging. You've already decided to take the journey, mapped out how to get to your destination and how you'll celebrate once you get there. Tell your "friends" with the negative advice, warnings, and attitudes to keep it to themselves. Only words of encouragement from here on out, and if they can't handle that—if they just can't be there for you as you work hard on you—they can take the same door as your bad habits. Tell them not to let the doorknob hit 'em where the good Lord split 'em.

GET RID OF THE WORD CAN'T. Seriously, you got this. The word *can't* cannot be a part of your vocabulary; you have to identify what you want and go for it, no matter how hard, no matter how scary, no matter who is or isn't in your corner, no matter that you're not sure what's waiting for you on the other side of the obstacles in your way—including yourself. Remind yourself that you're unstoppable. Do it often. Pray for strength, courage, and wisdom. Get quiet and visualize your wins. Trust yourself and have faith that your goals are not only attainable but already your victory.

WARRIOR WORK

List three major goals you have for your life or career. In what ways are you succeeding? In what ways are you hampering your own progress?

_____

_____

_____

_____

_____

_____

_____

_____

_____

_____

_____

_____

_____

_____

_____

_____

_____

_____

For each major goal, list five ways you can get out of your own way to fulfill your dreams.

_____

_____

_____

_____

_____

_____

_____

_____

_____

_____

_____

_____

_____

_____

_____

We each possess the capacity for self-development. We also possess the capacity for self-destruction. The path that we chose to take—to pursue lightness or darkness—is the story that we take to our graves.

—KILROY J. OLDSTER, ATTORNEY AND AUTHOR

5

MAKE PEACE OR DIE: REMEMBER YOU'RE A HUMAN BEING

THE WARRIOR CODE: PRINCIPLE #5

*Being human means you will make mistakes. And you
will make mistakes, because failure is God's way
of moving you in another direction.*

—OPRAH WINFREY, BUSINESSWOMAN

No one is perfect—not even the fiercest warriors. Start there. We're all going to make mistakes, miniscule and larger than life. Instinct is to duck and hide or proclaim as loudly as the voice can muster, "It's not my fault." But shifting blame or denying you had anything to do with it at all won't change the fact that something's gone wrong and you're the cause of it. Taking responsibility for your actions is the strongest possible statement you can make—for those watching you, but especially for yourself. Doing so does not make you look weak—it makes you human. The better humans are able to humble themselves, be vulnerable, admit they've screwed up, and put themselves on the road to forgiveness—not just forgiveness by those affected by the mistake but themselves, too.

I am a witness. Just as sure as the sun rises in the morning and makes room for the moon in the night sky, I came this close to sabotaging my entry into the Marines, the military branch that would break me down, build me up, shape me, and ultimately help turn me into a warrior.

No doubt, I had what it took to make it to Parris Island—at least the potential. Sixty-seven. That was my magic number—the score on my practice test that convinced my recruiter that I had what it took to be a Marine recruit. It was a full seventeen points higher than what was required of women to earn a spot, and almost twice the score required of men, and it would open the door for me to be one of the first females to go into combat. The crazy part was that I wasn't even trying all that hard to score big, and when I took the real test, I approached it much in the same way; the room where we tested was hot and crowded and way too quiet, and all I wanted was for the testing to be over. It just went on . . . and on . . . and on . . . and I was pencil-whipping through the pages, trying to finish up so I could break out of there and breathe in some cool Chicago air. I did what I could and, as luck would have it, excelled. I was so hyped about it that I couldn't think about much else besides getting ready for Parris Island, where I'd spend six weeks in boot camp, then head into the life I'd dreamed, traveling the world as a Marine. I couldn't wait to wave two fingers at Chicago and be on my way.

As my final step into the service, I took my physical and passed with flying colors. Then came the wait: all I had to do was sit tight until it was time to head to Parris Island.

I spent that time connecting with this man I called myself in love with. I think about it now and I wonder what I was thinking—what he was thinking—that we thought it was a good idea to be together. He was twenty-three, six years my senior, with a few kids spread throughout Chicago. It didn't matter that he didn't have a job, that he didn't have a car, that he had no real relationship with his children, that he was way too old and mature for my seventeen-year-old self. In my eyes, he was everything, and I . . . oh my goodness, I was in love. I spent the majority of my days before checking in for boot camp riding the bus over to his place, just to spend my days lying up under him, smoking marijuana, and listening to his lies. "We're going to get married," he'd say, "and have a bunch of babies. A family. You'll see."

And I believed him because that is what seventeen-year-olds do when grown men are talking to them about grown-up things. In my mind, he was a gift. Perfect.

It never occurred to me, though, that what I'd imagined as pure perfection would turn into my worst nightmare. With visions of us being together forever in my head, I shipped off for boot camp ready to start my adventure, excited that by the time I got out of boot camp, I'd become a Marine right around the time that all my friends graduated high school, and confident that my man would be waiting for me when I got back home. Suitcase in hand, I said goodbye to him, my sisters, and my mother and traveled almost two hours to the Naval Station Great Lakes Military Entrance Processing Station.

Unbeknownst to me, I had to submit to one final physical before heading off to boot camp; I thought nothing of taking this test, getting that shot, peeing in the cup, waiting in the room for the go-ahead to get on the bus. But when every person in that room started getting called out one by one, and I kept listening for my name and it wasn't called until I was the absolute last person in that room, I knew something wasn't right. That was confirmed when, finally, a woman calmly walked in my direction and said, rather casually, "Did you know you were pregnant?"

I'm sure I saw stars. A thunderclap of fear ricocheted off my heart, past my lungs, down to the pit of my stomach as I recycled the news: I had a baby in my belly.

"No, I didn't know," I stammered, absentmindedly looking down at my suitcase.

"Well, obviously, going to boot camp is out. Let me get your recruiter on the phone, see about getting you a ride back home."

That drive, with my recruiter at the wheel, was the longest ride ever—two hours of travel that felt like twenty. I dreaded walking back through my mother's front door just hours after we'd said our teary goodbyes and she hugged me close and told me how proud she was of me. I left the house with my nose held high and my shoulders squared, ready to start my new life and happy that, finally, I was making it out of Chicago, and just as quickly as I'd left, I had to stand in front of my mom and tell her that, once again, I'd messed up.

Within an hour of sharing the news with my mother, my sisters arrived—first Dorothy, then Patricia. And then the high-level war room discussions began, with each of them leaning in, putting their heads together, and considering my options. They had, it seemed, only one: I would have an abortion.

I went along with the decision, sure, but mostly because it felt like I had no other choice. I had no job, no money, with neither a pot to pee in nor a window to throw it out of. How was I going to care for a baby? Who was going to help me? The man who'd gotten me pregnant already had a bunch of children he wasn't really capable of taking care of; I didn't trust that he would step up for my baby when he hadn't done so for all the others. Plus, I would never make it in the Marines with a newborn—never make it off my block, much less out of Chicago. Having an abortion was the best option. The only option, really.

I REMEMBER MY ABORTION IN SNIPPETS: I remember the ride to the clinic. I remember checking in and hearing my name called. I remember lying on the table and being out of it. I remember being scared. I remember waking up in the recovery room. I remember someone shoving apple juice, graham crackers, and water toward me and telling me to eat and drink. I remember sitting there for what seemed like an eternity, covered with a heavy blanket, shivering and staring at this little TV in the corner of the sitting room. I remember floating in and out of consciousness. I remember being anxious. I remember being incredibly sad—empty. Like someone had taken a knife and carved a piece of me—limb, breast, lung, heart—off my body.

And then I was back home, in my mother's house. Having recuperated physically but not mentally from the surgery, I didn't reach out to anyone for at least a week—not even my boyfriend. I didn't know how he would feel about what I'd done, and I wasn't ready for him to find out. When I finally told him why I never made it to boot camp and was back in Chicago, he blew up, hollering and screaming and pissed that

I'd "killed his seed," and especially that I did it behind his back. Needless to say, that relationship ended about as abruptly as it started. After that, I spiraled back into my old habits with the same people, in the same streets, but with a new guy who became my fix. My plan to go to the Marines: dead. My dream of leaving Chicago, an inescapable nightmare: over. Soon enough, the days separating me from my original boot camp start date turned into weeks, then months, and, finally, a distant memory.

It was my mother who snapped me out of my daze. She'd left me alone to mourn both the loss of my baby and failure at going to and successfully completing boot camp, but after a while, watching me mope around the house, beg for a little change (which she gave me, completely unaware that I was using it to buy liquor) and hang out in the street, and waste precious days doing nothing finally got to her. Of course, that led to yet another big talk.

"Come sit down next to me right here," she said, patting the sofa late one afternoon after I finally yawned myself awake and slunk past her into the kitchen, where I stood with the refrigerator door open, looking lazily for something to eat. Fully aware of what was coming, I slowly trudged over to the couch. "You're not working, you're not in school, you're not in the Marines. What do you plan on doing with yourself? Because you can't stay here and be like this. Not on my watch," she said, folding her arms. Her words were quiet but stern. "You need to pull it together and do something with yourself. You're not a baby anymore. You grown. It's time for you to act like it."

That was the talk I expected. And when I'm being honest

with myself, it's also the talk that I needed. In that one conversation, my mother managed to refocus my attention—to remind me that there was an incredible life waiting for me. All I had to do was take the first step.

By week's end, I was back at the recruiting station, reenlisting with the man who'd recruited my brother and me. Though I had to fill out all the paperwork again and take another physical fitness test, I was able to skip retaking the aptitude test, which made me almost jump for joy because, really, I couldn't bear the thought of holing up in that hot room and sweating over all those questions again. I did have to take the physical again, and this time, I wasn't pregnant. I left there that day feeling renewed, with a new ship date—December 8, 1996—on my calendar and a renewed sense of accomplishment. Finally, I was going to be on my way.

I was also going to have my fun before I shipped off.

With my new plans firmly in place, I did what any self-respecting party animal would do: I went out of my way to have a good time before shipping off. It was my cousins—one older, one younger—who helped me revel in the debauchery. We had a schedule that ran tighter than a Swiss watch: their mom, a security guard at the airport, would leave for work at noon. At exactly 12:01 P.M., I would be getting off the bus and walking to their house, and posting up on the couch with some marijuana in one hand and a cup of Malibu rum and pineapple juice in the other—that was our drink of choice. My aunt kept a huge bottle of Malibu in her cabinet, and we would drink it down like we were grown. Every day, it would be smoke weed, drink Malibu and pineapple juice, cut up potatoes and drop them in some hot oil for fresh french fries, then fill Auntie's Malibu bottle back up with water to the line she marked off with black ink (to make sure no one was drinking her liquor), and get down the road before she arrived home at 11:00 P.M. Every once in a while, if it was warm enough and we had enough cash between us, we would break the routine and head outside to see if we could give someone ten dollars to buy us malt liquor, because though we were all acting grown, none of us were actually old enough to cop our own alcoholic beverages. Between that and the Malibu, we were always lit.

This was especially so the night before I was to ship off to boot camp. My foolish logic: I should smoke as much weed and drink as much liquor as my body could stand before shipping off the next day, not only to celebrate my new station in life but also because it would be a long time before I'd be able to have my fun again. I was living for the moment. Being free.

Of course, choosing to be free almost cost me. Unbeknownst to me, all recruits who reported for boot camp had to undergo a drug test. Everybody else, it seemed, knew this but me. It was the talk that dominated the conversation among us recruits on the flight to Parris Island; the airplane was full of people who were doing the most to get the drugs out of their system before we landed—drinking special teas, taking supplements, downing mixtures of vinegar and honey and a bunch of other concoctions they'd heard would mask the drugs in their urine. As for me, I really didn't care. Not once did I think maybe I should've been drinking a ton of water or asking someone for a detox pill. In my mind, what was done was done and the Marines would either take me or send me home; there was nothing else I could do about that.

I did feel dread and an impending sense of doom, though, when they separated us into different groups, led us all into a room, and got in our faces about confessing our sins before we fully transitioned from civilian to military life. There was a lot of screaming and face-to-face connection—hot breath and spittle in our faces as the drill instructors drove home how much our lives were about to change and that we were about to belong to the Marines and that we'd better come clean if we'd done something we weren't supposed to have done.

"You'd better tell it now!" one of the drill instructors yelled in my face. "Because if we find out, you will be kicked out!"

Of course, no one wants to get kicked out of the military, as it comes with serious repercussions: a dishonorable discharge, which ruins one's ability to collect a laundry list of benefits available to veterans once they leave the military, and even military prison. The high-volume threats were a scare tactic, but they were working on me.

One drill instructor looked directly into my eyes like she could see clear down to my soul—like she knew I'd binged on weed and alcohol the night before without my even having told her. "Step up! Say it!"

Those of us who had something to confess and decided to come clean were instructed to stand up from our chairs and bear witness to our sins. Those who remained seated were escorted out of the room and to the squad bay, while those of us in the hot seats were ordered to, one by one, tell what we'd done.

"What did you do?" the drill instructor demanded, leaning into my face close enough for me to see the shine on her molars.

"I smoked weed the night before," I said without hesitation.

She glared at me, ordered me to sit back down, and moved on to the next person, working her way around the room as recruits told all their business. It was the moment of truth for all of us.

I was shaking, wondering if they'd put me back on a bus to Chicago; finally, an immense amount of regret was threatening to swallow me whole. The stakes were high, and I was trying hard to steel myself for the price I'd have to pay for my actions. Clammy, scared, and staring straight ahead, I awaited my fate in the dead silence of the room. Then, finally, the drill instructors started circulating between the chairs, laying sheets of paper down in front of us transgressors.

"I need you to read over the paperwork, write down what you did, and sign the waiver," the drill instructor said. "This releases the Marines from any liability should your actions result in any kind of injury or harm during basic training. You will acknowledge that it is your personal responsibility."

I felt like someone had used a pin to release the pressure that had crowded in my stomach and head while I awaited my fate. Confessing—owning up to what I'd done—was hard, but knowing that I'd come clean and made it to the other side of that door felt good. Right.

And when I marched out into the open air—into that cold winter air—I knew for sure this time that my life would never, ever be the same.

I did not set out to get pregnant, and I certainly didn't think about the ramifications of having drugs in my system on the day that I was to start boot camp. I chalk up both decisions to a tactless lack of judgment—a mixture of youthful indiscretion, a devil-may-care attitude about the connection between choices and consequences, and an immature notion about what love is. But I can admit that I was the architect of each of those choices, each of which could have ended in disaster: I could have become a teen single mother, starting my own leg of a cycle of poverty that gripped so many families in my community, or I could have been kicked out of boot camp and sent back to Chicago, where, surely, I would have continued on down the destructive path I was on, drinking, smoking weed, and imbedding myself more deeply into gang culture.

Thank goodness that even in the midst of my self-destruction, even at the tender age of seventeen, I understood that my life and the intentions I had for it didn't have to end. Of course, I had the encouragement, support, and, perhaps most importantly, a serious push from my mom and sister, who were infinitely wiser than I when it came to seeing where my destructive path would lead me. But ultimately, I had to take responsibility for my actions and make the decisions that would help me get back to what I saw for myself—to get back to my ultimate play. I knew that my freedom and my ability to be the warrior I envisioned becoming was wholly dependent on a series of actions that would right the wrongs I'd done to myself.

Young, old, rich, poor, whatever color, whatever background, literally everyone makes mistakes. But not all of us stand at the ready to admit their missteps to themselves or others. It's embarrassing. It's a sign that you're not perfect. And it takes work to correct the mistake—work that requires one to stretch mentally, emotionally, physically, even, in some cases, financially. And you still run the risk that whatever you've done wrong won't right itself despite your coming clean. With all that at stake, it's tempting after making a mistake to play it off like you didn't make one—or to shirk the responsibilities that come with it. But owning your mistakes—admitting you did something wrong, taking responsibility for your actions, and committing to doing better going forward—is a true sign of strength, courage, and wisdom, the kind that shows growth and ultimately boosts your self-worth.

I know that in my case, admitting to smoking marijuana the night before I headed to Parris Island for boot camp was scary as hell, but it felt right. Coming clean earned—rather than cost—me a spot in the boot camp. I was able to keep going because I was honest about what I'd done and stood ready to accept the consequences of my actions. Had I sat there and pretended like I led a holy and sanctified life leading up to that very moment, and then a drug test revealed otherwise, my lie would have sent me packing back to Chicago.

Warriors don't slink away with their tails between their legs, too scared, stubborn, or stupid to fess up to their mess. Instead, they stand tall, square their shoulders, admit the mistake, fix the wrong, and fight to get what they want and need—the right way. Here's how warriors own their mistakes:

1. **They apologize.** I'm not talking about the knee-jerk automated "I'm sorry" your mother forced you to say as a kid when you slapped your little brother or snatched a toy from a playmate; I'm talking that grown-up apology that genuinely acknowledges you've done something wrong and someone was hurt by it. This requires laying excuses to the side, truly deliberating and understanding why you're at fault, lifting the

blame onto your own shoulders, and saying, from deep down in your gut, that you're owning what you did and are genuinely sorry about it. There will be no true healing without it. You'll have to employ that humbleness I talked about earlier, recognizing that someone was hurt by your actions and can only be made whole by your being a bigger person and working hard to make the person you hurt whole. This does not make you weak. Indeed, extending a sincere apology is a profound example of good character, one of the most important traits of a strong warrior. Note: the injured party isn't obligated to accept your apology or even warm up to you after accepting it. Sometimes getting over the hurt takes a minute. Give the aggrieved party the space he or she needs, but know that a sincere apology is a salve for the wound you created.

2.   They forgive themselves. This was a huge one for me. We're consistently taught the value of forgiveness: accepting someone's apology (or moving on from a bad situation even when the person who hurt us refuses to acknowledge his or her digs) releases us from the shackles of anger and bitterness and propels us back toward the light. There is power in the release. We get bigger. But showing ourselves grace doesn't come nearly as easily. We're trained practically from birth to be incredibly self-critical and to beat ourselves up if we do wrong. We are always our own biggest critics. This was certainly true when I found out I was pregnant just as I was about to make my big getaway. Granted, I wasn't being careful with the man I was having sex with, and I really did not give the consequences of unprotected sex the thought it deserved. To be fair, I was seventeen—a kid—and thought I was in love, for no other reason than that we hung in the same crowd, liked to do the same destructive things, and he liked me back. I wasn't thinking about the fact that he already had several kids with different mothers and the relationships he had with the latter were fraught. I certainly wasn't thinking about whether he would be a good father to our child if we made one. I wasn't considering, either, how my life would change having to care for a baby at such a young age, with no money, no resources, no home of my own—nothing. Having a baby would have been a game changer for me; it likely would have relegated me to a lot of dreams deferred. Having an abortion, then, was the smart thing to do. The right thing. It was saving my life. Still, I felt so much guilt over the procedure; what kind of person was I that I could rid my body of a life I'd helped to create? What would it have been—boy? Girl? Would I have been a decent enough mother? Could my baby have grown up to be someone important? Or could he or she have ended up struggling through childhood like I had, wondering about his or her place in the world? I felt such a tremendous amount of guilt as I considered each of these things, and I beat myself up for being in the predicament in the first place—for forcing my own hand in planning my parenthood and putting on hold my plans to join the Marines. It took me quite a bit of time to really reconcile what I'd done and even longer to forgive myself for getting in the predicament in the first place, much less aborting my baby. Getting there took serious work—a constant conversation with myself about how life is made up of choices and I'd made the right one for myself. Not for anyone else but myself.

3.   They learn from it. Mistakes are going to happen. This is life. It's as constant as the passing of time. Feeling stupid, embarrassed, or ashamed for making them is natural, too. But folding into yourself and hiding after you make one—or one hundred!—won't make things better or right. Squaring your shoulders, holding your head up high, and embracing the lessons you've learned from your mistakes are what make you grow. They're what make you strong. Plus, at the very least, you learn what *not* to do again, meaning you get wiser, too, as you workshop ways to perfect what you set out to do in the first place. There isn't a successful entrepreneur on the planet who made it to the top without first making mistakes and using what he or she learned to make changes that would ultimately put him or her in the black. Personal mistakes work the same way: a bad breakup hurts like hell when you're going through it, but going into that next relationship, you're pretty clear about what you will and won't tolerate from the new guy and know a lot better what you need to feel happy and whole. The key is to be honest with yourself about what went wrong, and be thoughtful about what you need to do to move forward.

FIFTEEN WAYS YOU CAN LEARN FROM A MISTAKE AND TURN IT INTO A WIN

1. Now you'll know whom to trust and who gets the flat hand when they look in your direction.

2. Now you'll know what you're passionate about.

3. Now you'll know your weaknesses and in which areas you need to build your muscle.

4. Change is coming—and that's a good thing.

5. You'll know a little bit more about yourself and the amount of pressure you can withstand.

6. You'll know a little bit more about the people surrounding you and how much pressure they can take.

7. Humility is delivered by the truckload.

8. You made it through the storm, and now you'll see just how strong you really are.

9. Now you're inspired to be even better at whatever it was you failed at.

10. And you'll make better choices because, right now, you know better than anyone all the little mistakes you made along the way that led to the big mistake.

11. Plus, you'll see what really matters to you and what's a waste of brain matter.

12. Congrats: now you know you're human!

13. That skill set is about to be hella elevated.

14. And you've got some goals laid out. Plans are a good thing.

15. You know for sure how to respond to the next mistake. And yes, you will make more mistakes. Many more, in fact. And that's okay.

WARRIOR WORK

Write down four mistakes you've made in the past year, plus how you responded to them. What would you do differently?

_____

_____

_____

_____

_____

_____

_____

_____

_____

*Mistakes are always forgivable, if one has the courage
to admit them.*

—BRUCE LEE, ACTOR

6

ALWAYS FAITHFUL, ALWAYS FORWARD: DON'T QUIT

THE WARRIOR CODE: PRINCIPLE #6

Many of life's failures are people who did not realize how close they were to success when they gave up.

—THOMAS EDISON, SCIENTIST AND INVENTOR

Look, failure happens, despite our best intentions and efforts. But that doesn't mean you have to give up. I like to think of failure as a natural stop on the road to success. Each time you go back to the task at hand, you get a little better, a little wiser, a bit more seasoned in ways that only help you move closer to acing what you're tackling. You have to put your failures to work to get to the success, but you simply cannot get to the success if you give up and accept failure as the punctuation on your journey. You have to dig deep into your reserve of self-discipline, focus on what you need to hit your targets, and hold tight to a deep faith that all your hard work, all your preparation, and yes, every last one of your failures will ultimately help you to succeed. Quitting simply cannot ever be in your arsenal.

At boot camp, quitting always felt like it was on the table for someone. There was always some girl in her rack late at night, crying about how hard it was. The tough-as-nails transition began the moment each of us stepped our toes off the bus and onto those yellow footprints on which we had to line up: we were stripped of all we had except for the clothes on our backs and taught in the toughest ways possible how to build ourselves back up. There was a lot of yelling—the drill instructors took pride in disciplining us recruits for even the littlest of things—and zero tolerance for disrespect. One's voice could go hoarse from yelling, "Yes, sir!" and "No, ma'am!" for every single, solitary little thing, and it was an adjustment, to say the least, to lose complete autonomy over daily moments we take for granted. Something as simple as taking a shower came with detailed instructions: line up, march to the showerhead, pull the ring to wet your head, soap your head and face, rinse, soap your left arm, rinse, soap your right arm, rinse—in that order. Something as simple as making your bed—or, as it's called in the service, your *rack*—incorrectly could get you chewed out; taking too long in the bathroom could get you chewed out; wearing your field gear or uniform wrong could get you chewed out and disciplined with physical punishment—push-ups, lots of barking and spittle in your face, running, more push-ups. And somewhere in there, we had to prove our physical endurance—meeting specific run times and hitting certain marks on flex arm hangs and sit-ups.

And that was just during phase one.

"Forming," the first few days designed to get us ready for basic training, was like being dropped directly into an inferno. That's when we learned how to wear our uniforms, secure our weapons, and march, plus learn an entirely new way of talking:

we were never, ever to refer to ourselves as *me* or *I* or *them* and *us*. We were recruits, and the others were *those recruits*. Upstairs was *topside*; the floor was a *deck*; the ceiling was an *overhead*. And when you answered a drill instructor, you'd better yell loud enough for your tonsils to catch fire, because meek and timid would only get you into more trouble.

It was a whole new way of talking, of living—of being.

By the time we made it into week-four training, there were plenty of women surrounding me who were shaken. They'd cry after being yelled at, cry if they were being worked hard, cry if they were missing their families and friends. Mostly, I laughed at them and the situations we found ourselves in; they were weak, and boot camp wasn't that hard, really. Not to shortchange the importance and seriousness of boot camp, but I'd already gone through military school: I'd already faced people screaming at me, I already knew how to make my rack a very specific way, I already was accustomed to the ungodly wake-up times, I knew how to wear a uniform, I was still in shape from all the running and push-ups and military drills I'd done at the school. I was prepared for boot camp, mentally and physically. So what was happening during my official entry into the Marines was laughable to me. Like, I literally laughed my way through it.

Now granted, this also was my way with most things, particularly when it came to dealing with authority. Remember the time when I got arrested for stealing from the school lockers and I laughed my way through the interrogation until my sister Dorothy retrieved me? When I think about it as an adult, I recognize that my response was rooted not just in a devil-may-care attitude but also an extreme coping mechanism for personal trauma. I'd already fought my way through two false starts getting into the military—an abortion and a last-minute drug scare—to get to Parris Island; I felt like there wasn't anything that could turn me around. I had nothing to be scared of; I'd come from the streets of the South Side of Chicago, where there was plenty more to be frightened of than some woman yelling and spitting in my face, and I'd already faced down the drill instructors and their nighttime obstacle courses at military school. I knew I had the smarts to be there; my test scores proved that much. And when it came to physical skill, I took great pleasure in acing the challenges. I'm tall—five feet nine inches—and strong, and when it came time to hump on ten-mile hikes, I carried the SAW, a portable machine gun that was as heavy as it was powerful, because I could. I raised my hand for that work.

Still, I wasn't the best recruit. I drove the drill instructors crazy because there's nothing worse than not being able to break down a recruit who is too relaxed or takes every serious moment like some kind of joke. It seemed like every day, sometimes two or three times a day, it would be me cracking a joke, the recruits standing next to me giggling, and then, "Recruit Hudson! Give me forty push-ups, now!" from a drill instructor. But no number of push-ups and no amount of yelling could break me; I could handle the physical punishment, nothing any of them said to me could make me cry, and any task they gave got completed exceptionally. This made me a problem. I wasn't playing the game the way the Marines needed me to play it, and they couldn't drop or recycle me because outside of being an unapologetic jerky jokester, I wasn't doing anything wrong.

Soon enough, though, the drill instructors figured out how to break me, using what was my personal kryptonite: loyalty.

Despite always being in trouble, I managed to curry favor with my platoon precisely because of my personality. I was still tough as nails, but in a platoon, our mission was to bond with one another as if our very lives depended on it. The fact of the matter is that in combat, on the field, we need to move as one to complete missions and come out of it intact, so training us to do that in boot camp was paramount. That part of our mission as recruits resonated with me because of the way I grew up in back in Chicago; growing up on the 9, you were loyal to the people who pledged to have your back, no matter what. That is how you stayed alive. That is how you collected people who were charged with keeping you alive. Doing so was critical.

And so it wasn't a thing for me to extend that thinking in boot camp. We were our own gang, and I was happy to be a part of it. At night, I'd put on puppet shows with socks, making fun of the drill instructors under the glare of my flashlight when we were all supposed to be sleeping. I was big on sharing, too; we were in a platoon where this was allowed, and so whenever my mother sent my favorite snack to me— multiple bags of Flamin' Hot Cheetos—I'd give until the bags were gone. Soon enough, we clung to our drill instructors' insistence that the other platoons were our mortal enemies and that we needed to depend on and trust only those in our platoon. After that, we were inseparable.

But then, a month and a half into building our sisterhood, the drill instructors flipped the script on me.

"Hudson!" my drill instructor yelled one morning while we were busy getting ready for the day.

I double-timed it over to her, stood at attention, and yelled, "Yes, ma'am!"

"Pack all your crap! You're moving to Platoon 4009."

My heart jumped as if it were about to push through my chest and splatter on the floor between us. It was the same feeling I'd had when, in the beginning of my high school career, my family moved from our neighborhood into rival gang territory, and I was left to fend for myself—a sheep among wolves who stood at the ready to eat me alive. I wanted desperately to scream, "But why?" and "I don't want to go over there—they're the enemy!" But talking back like that wasn't an option. My sole response had to be, "Aye, ma'am!"

Tears welled in my eyes. The drill instructor smirked; I could see the satisfaction pulsing in her eyes. Finally, she'd broken me.

I gathered my belongings, neatly but quickly tossed them into my duffel bags—with the assistance of a few other recruits—took one last look around our platoon, and marched out the door and over to the neighboring squad bay, the rival platoon. Once again, I was a sheep among wolves.

I QUICKLY PULLED MYSELF together before I walked into my new platoon; there was no way I was going to let them see me cry. I replaced that emotion with anger. This was enemy territory, but being in the enemy's den was something I'd experienced before. I was given the last empty rack and assigned Recruit Smith as my new bunkmate. For the first two days, very few people engaged in conversation with me; others would just steal glances every now and then. There I was again, somewhere I didn't belong.

There were no more jokes from me—there was no more attitude. The move had cut me deeply, and from then on out, I was all business, taking what was being poured into me much more seriously. My first mission was to get comfortable in my new platoon. Granted, this was the most awkward of all because I was arriving from a rival platoon with zero trust for the new women I was charged with forging a bond with, and I missed the women from my original platoon, whom I'd already loved as sisters. I was forbidden to communicate with them—though I did sneak a few quick conversations here and there, because that's where my heart still was. Instead, I poured myself into learning how to trust these new women and programmed my mind to think of them as my sisters. In some ways, it felt like I was some kind of spy, lurking where I didn't belong, gathering information I didn't have any business knowing, working two different angles for some benefit—for the greater good of the boot camp. But eventually, I came to look at the new platoon as my sisters, too. They weren't as nasty as my old drill instructors had been telling us—nowhere near as horrible as they'd proclaimed. Soon enough, we were sisters, too, and I became the glue between the two platoons that were supposed to hate one another.

Getting acclimated with my new platoon was the easy part, though. To win the game, I needed to win over the drill instructors. And myself. See, they'd begun to tell me that I wasn't going to make it—that I wasn't cut out to be a Marine. "You're not going to make it in a fleet," they insisted. "You're not even going to last your first enlistment. You'll be putting in your papers, begging to get out."

It was a mind trick to keep me in my place, to break me all

the way down to build me all the way back up by making me prove myself and my worth. This was the toughest of all for me because I'd already been hearing from my brother that I wasn't tough enough to be a Marine, and now, here I was, hearing those same words on the tongues of the drill instructors. I'm not going to lie: they had me believing it, too. I even started thinking maybe I'd joined the wrong branch, particularly when I bumped up against my biggest obstacles: learning how to swim and becoming a skilled marksman.

I had no clue until a couple of weeks prior to my first day at boot camp that I would have to meet swim qualifications. I arrived to boot camp unable to hold my own in the water. Learning to swim, after all, was not a priority on the South Side of Chicago. We didn't live in houses with private swimming pools, my mother wasn't laying out precious nickels and dimes to put me through swim lessons, and hanging out at the community pool wasn't an option, because it wasn't what my friends and I did; we didn't have the resources to swim. So when I was told I'd have to learn, I was scared. And as much as I wanted to pick it up, I sucked at it; it was the one thing I could never master. Those of us who couldn't swim were given extra remedial time while the rest of the platoon got through qualifications and went on to the next boot camp requirement. Even more of a challenge: I was learning basic swim strokes, floating techniques, and how to survive in water, all while wearing a full combat load, including a rifle, a helmet, boots, a flak jacket, and a pack. I just couldn't do it. I was one of two women who didn't pass the swim test; I ended up having to spend an extra week in remedial training.

I had a problem with target practice, too. I'd held a gun

before I went to boot camp; growing up in the streets of Chicago will make that possible for any kid looking to do so. I'd never actually shot a gun, but I did quite well during practice week. The training was extensive: in addition to memorizing the rules of weapons safety and learning the proper marksman techniques, we had to learn the four standard Marine Corps firing positions, plus how to adjust our sights, adjust our shooting according to different weather conditions, and, most importantly, know for sure how to hit our target. All of this led up to firing week, where we fired our weapons for the first time, using all we'd learned. Our first charge was targets, and then we had to complete an actual course to qualify, firing fifty rounds worth up to 5 points. To pass the course, recruits had to earn a minimum of 190 points out of 250 points to get a Marine Corps marksmanship badge. To qualify as a sharpshooter or an expert, recruits had to earn 210 and 200 points, respectively.

When it came to qualifications day, though, I hit a wall: my drill instructor. For some reason, I was the focus of her hostility that morning, and while, for the most part, the drill instructor had pretty much up to that point left us alone during our marksmanship classes with the instructor, that day, I was in her crosshairs. Just before the official test, I was pitted—a term we Marines use when we're made to do push-ups, flutter kicks, mountain climbers, and whatever other quick-fire punishment the drill instructors could make us do in what we'd nicknamed "the hell pit." Two hours later, I received news that I'd unqualified on the rifle range. And that meant I wasn't going to graduate, as this was a requirement before one made it out of boot camp and became a full-fledged

Marine. I'd never felt lower than when I saw my score. Here I was, a failure, with my brother's words ringing in my ears. He was right: I wasn't cut out to be a Marine.

But I refused to give up. I had my pride.

The next day, when I got a second chance to qualify, that same drill instructor walked over to me and offered words of encouragement—words that rang in my ears as I took and passed both my swim and rifle range qualifications.

Once I settled that score, I had to conquer one more mission to become official: the Crucible, a fifty-four-hour test of our physical, mental, and moral fortitude. Every last recruit had to successfully complete the Crucible to become a Marine.

Honestly, it is a blur to me. I remember the first night being awakened and ordered to march for what seemed like days, one foot in front of the other as each of us struggled to see into the distance and figure out just where they were taking us. That was probably the closest I've ever come to sleep-walking. All I can remember is drifting in and out of sleep until we got to our destination, where more fresh hell awaited.

I'd made it: I'd fought through the emotions, the challenges, the failures, and the doubt and did what I needed to do to win. I persisted. Finally, I was a Marine. When a recruit finally passes the Crucible, she is given an eagle globe and anchor from her drill instructor to symbolize the moment and solidify the fact that she is now no longer a recruit but a Marine. I cried when I received mine—the first time I let my tears flow in boot camp.

Truly, it was the one thing I'd desired most of all. Well, that and the support of my family. Unfortunately, the latter failed to materialize on graduation day: my mother couldn't make it. In fact, the only person from my family who came was Dorothy. In that sea of bleachers, with families cheering and waving flowers and showing by their mere presence that they were proud of their newly minted Marines, I was standing there, the adopted girl from Chicago, having accomplished something major—having conquered every challenge thrown my way—feeling like a motherless child. In those moments, I was reminded of who I was. For better and for worse. But I was determined to shine.

I didn't get into boot camp to quit—to give up and go home and lick my wounds and spiral back into all the things I wanted desperately to leave behind. I was intent on getting bigger—on following through on my promise to myself to become a Marine, travel the world, and make a difference for not only myself but also for my country. Giving up wasn't an option. The sole way to reach my goal was to dig deep into my well of persistence—that dogged determination to accomplish exactly what I'd set out to do.

Of course, when I drew from that well, my bucket was heavy as hell and full of obstacles: self-doubt, fear of failure, shame, concern over how others perceived my talents and abilities. But I put my head down, did the work, and reminded myself often that I'm not a quitter. Quitting is not what warriors do.

From here on out, it's not going to be what you do, either. Here's how you're going to build that persistence muscle so you can face down those obstacles and meet your goals:

1. **Visualize your goal.** What do you want? A fit body? A promotion? To play the piano? A house to call your own?

Picture yourself having exactly what you want—literally. Rip out a magazine picture of your dream house or find an old picture of yourself from when you thought you looked good in that dress or bathing suit, and stick it somewhere where you will see it every day—your bathroom mirror, your computer screen. You can even make the song you want to learn how to play on the piano your morning alarm clock music. Whatever the goal, however you choose to display it, make it so that you can actually see it so that you can keep your eyes on the prize.

2. Make an action plan. Every goal has steps to achieving it. Get yourself a notebook and write down the exact actions it'll take for you to reach your goal. To get to your dream weight, maybe it's hiring a trainer, agreeing to work out at least four days a week for an hour, upping your intake of water, and eating a specific low-carb, low-sugar diet. Buying a house might involve checking your credit score, getting approved for a mortgage, identifying neighborhoods you'd like to live in, and hiring a real estate agent. Putting the steps that'll lead to your goal on paper will make them more real and even more achievable if you show yourself that the steps aren't all that hard.

3. Get yourself a cheerleader. A big part of my being able to go back at the weapons training and swimming qualifications was because I was surrounded by fellow recruits who had my back and wouldn't let me quit or fail. It's true: you have to depend on yourself, first and foremost, to see your goals through. No one can work out for you, or keep you from buying those new shoes when you're supposed to be saving money, or take that continuing education class if you're looking to boost your credentials for that job promotion; these are steps toward your goal that you have to do on your own. But there's nothing like having a friend or two, or a mentor or trainer, to see you through the tough times, whether as companions joining you on the journey or accountability partners charged with checking in on your progress and pushing you to stay motivated, determined, and intent on reaching that goal. This is your "Yes, You Can" team—the ones who will fight for you, ride with you, and push you when you're on the edge of giving up. Bonus if that squad has already done what you're looking to do: they come with sound advice on how to achieve your goals and avoid the mistakes that might stop you in your tracks.

4.   Dive in and make it a routine. Get to work and go hard as you move step by step through the action plan you've laid out for yourself. Make a point of working toward your goal every day—no matter what. Make it a priority by scheduling it into your day: know that every day during your 3:00 P.M. break, you will stand up at your desk, put on your sneakers, stretch, and walk up three flights of stairs at work, or each night before dinner, you'll memorize and practice saying at least twenty new French words. Sunday afternoons could be reserved for preparing and packing healthy lunches for the week. Don't forget to have fun with it! Make yourself a workout playlist, or have your kids test your new language skills; hinging something you love on a challenging task makes it easier to get through.

5.   Track your progress. You know where you started: you've weighed yourself or made note of how much of a down payment you need for that new house. Jot that down in a journal or on a calendar, then set small, measurable goals to keep track of as you get to work. Maybe that means you step on the scale every Friday and write down how much your weight has changed, or you track how fast your run around the block was this week compared to last. Marking a calendar with a simple note saying, "Yes, you ate three servings of vegetables and drank a half gallon of water today," would make a great reminder that you're working hard and will realize the rewards sooner rather than later.

6.   Treat yourself. Do this not just at the end of your journey when you've reached your goal; give yourself rewards for small, measurable goals along the way to propel yourself forward. We all know, after all, that the biggest challenge for meeting a goal, particularly if it's a long-range goal, is staying motivated. To keep yourself from burning out, dole out small rewards to yourself to keep yourself on the grind. Work out for at least four days a week and reward yourself with a movie; do this for four weeks straight and you could earn yourself a professional massage. Bigger goals reap bigger rewards. How's that French coming? Reach a certain level of proficiency and promise yourself a trip to a country where you can practice your newfound skills. Whatever it is you choose to do, let the rewards inspire you to keep going.

WARRIOR WORK

Here's where you put that action plan in motion. What is your biggest goal right now? Write it down.

_____

_____

_____

_____

_____

_____

_____

_____

Write specific steps you'll need to take to achieve that goal, plus deadlines for completing each of those steps.

_____

_____

_____

_____

_____

_____

_____

_____

_____

Write the names and contact information for your cheerleaders who will help you achieve the goal. For instance, if your goal is to lose weight, write down the name of a nutritionist, a personal trainer, and a gym where you plan to exercise.

_____

_____

_____

_____

_____

_____

_____

_____

_____

_____

_____

_____

Finally, write down at least three ways you'll treat yourself once you hit your goal.

_____

_____

_____

_____

_____

_____

_____

_____

_____

_____

_____

_____

Difficulties break some men but make others. No axe is sharp enough to cut the soul of a sinner who keeps on trying, one armed with the hope that he will rise even in the end.

—NELSON MANDELA, SOUTH AFRICAN ANTIAPARTHEID LEADER

7

SEMPER FI (WITH COURAGE): BE BRAVE

THE WARRIOR CODE: PRINCIPLE #7

Be convinced that to be happy means to be free and that to be free means to be brave.

—THUCYDIDES, GREEK GENERAL AND HISTORIAN

To me, bravery and the pursuit of happiness are deeply intertwined. That's because choosing happiness is never, ever as easy as it sounds. Doing so requires you to tune out critics who can't see what you see for yourself. Doing so requires you to let go of the sure thing and brace yourself for discomfort as you build your "new and improved" from scratch. Doing so requires you to get off your butt and hustle hard, even on days when your entire being craves the easier days when checks were steady, companionship was certain, and love was staring you in the face every night.

Doing so requires courage. A lot of it.

Being a warrior requires us to bravely let go of comfort and know that choosing to be happy is less an immediate achievement, much more a journey toward a goal. This is true in all aspects of life, whether you're bravely pursuing career satisfaction within a job environment that tends to be more toxic than rewarding, or struggling to leave a long-term romantic relationship, or trying to mend an important friendship that, on most days, feels like it's run its course. Breakups hurt. Walking away from a toxic job is scary. Deciding to distance yourself from a longtime friend who means you no good is heartbreaking. But sticking around out of fear is so much harder than suiting up, walking through the fire, healing, and going after exactly what you want for yourself. Wanting—really wanting—something for yourself is a helluva motivator. Fear isn't an option. When you make your pursuit of happiness your sole focus and you brave whatever getting free tosses your way, it pays off in spades.

I know this intimately. My first marriage lasted less than a year. I thought I was in love, he cheated on me, we fussed and fought until I just couldn't take it anymore, and then we were divorced. It was that much of a blur. But I remember the lessons—the ones that made me a stronger woman and mother. The lessons that grew me up. I owe that to becoming a Marine, certainly, but even more so to becoming a mother.

I was stationed in North Carolina, in the middle of an incredibly rocky relationship with my then boyfriend Carlo, when I found out I was pregnant. I didn't even know it, but somehow, my sergeant did. I had just completed a PFT, having just finished the run portion. When I crossed the finish line I puked up an orange substance. Apparently, that's what tipped her off, but Sergeant Cynthia Douglas insisted on escorting me to medical for a pregnancy test. At first, I resisted.

"Come on. My period comes like clockwork. I'd be the first one to know if something was off," I said.

"Well, if there's no baby in your belly, you have nothing to worry about."

Of course, it was much more than that. A navy medical service member in a white lab coat confirmed what my sergeant had suspected: I was going to be a mom.

I was devastated by the news. It had been just a few months earlier, after all, that I'd begun to confirm what my gut knew to be true: that Carlo was no good for me. That was when I'd found out that my then boyfriend had hit on one of my very best friends, Amy. From what I understand, nothing actually happened between them—no kissing, no sex—but I was devastated by the idea that the man who'd said he was committed to me could betray me in such a way with a woman whose friendship I treasured, and angry, too, that my best friend didn't hip me to the news. In fact, it was her boyfriend who called and dropped the gem: "Carlo's been pushing up on your girl," he said. "I just thought you should know how foul your boyfriend and best friend are."

Carlo and I fought about it, of course, and declaring her as having broken the ultimate girl code and not telling on herself, I stopped talking to my then best friend. Still, Carlo and I had found enough common ground somewhere over two months of fighting to make a baby, and there I was, standing in the middle of medical, staring at the medic in sheer terror. By the time I made it back to my unit, I was in a full panic. "Oh my God, what am I going to do?" I kept saying over and over again. How could I have a baby with a man with whom I couldn't get along? How would I even begin to carry out my duties as a Marine with a baby in my belly? Where would I find the money, time, and help to care for a child with everyone I knew, loved, and who supported me all the way up north in Chicago? Like when I was pregnant at age seventeen, every scenario flashed across my mind—adoption, abortion, keeping the baby, finding a happily ever after—but every last one of them scared me more than the others.

Before I could process—and, more importantly, check my emotions—another sergeant, a direct supervisor in my unit, pulled up next to my desk. Her normal 5'5" frame seemed to tower over me—she was an imposing figure—as I crumpled my forehead into my hands and choked back tears. She had fire in her eyes.

"Look," she snarled, leaning so close to my face I could smell her breath, "just because you're pregnant, don't think you're going to get special attention. Don't think you're not going to have to clean up like everyone else or complete your missions or get your work done." Tears welled up in my eyes, but that didn't stop my sergeant from leaning in a little closer and continuing her tirade. "I don't ever want to hear you complaining or saying anything about morning sickness, either, or how you're cramping or your feet are swollen," she continued.

Embarrassed, my eyes darted around the office; everyone, it seemed, was leaning in to hear the sergeant tear into me. My fear quickly turned into anger; here I was, grappling with this fresh news, and already, she was breaking me down, playing out some ridiculously bad cliché of a boss stuck in outdated stereotypes of working women. Clearly, she did not ascribe to the modern feminist belief that working women *can* do it all, and she was making clear that I would get extra scrutiny for daring to start a family on her watch. I could tell by the curl of the lip that she meant business.

Thankfully, Sergeant Douglas, who was in the next office

over, heard everything and made quick work of defending me. Before I could get in a word, she was in the evil supervisor's face. The argument was loud, rowdy, and uncomfortable.

"How dare you talk to her like that!" Sergeant Douglas said tersely. "She literally just found out she's pregnant, and this is what you have to offer her? Can she digest the information first? This is supposed to be your Marine. Your job is to support her, not chastise her. How about you talk to her? Try mentoring her? What are you doing?" She turned to me and said in a much gentler voice, "Go home. Take the rest of the day."

I quickly gathered my things and hightailed it out of the office, their loud arguing punctuating my every step until I was on the other side of the door, down the walkway, and out into the open air.

Sergeant Douglas was exactly whom I needed at that precise moment—someone who understood the stakes but had firsthand experience being both a mother and a Marine and knew, for sure, that a woman was capable of being both. She was married with two children of her own, and from that very moment, she became my savior. If it was lunchtime, she would take me out to eat and use the time during the car ride to school me on the ways of melding motherhood with being in the service. She minced no words.

"Your first priority is to your child. I need you to be really clear about that," she'd say as she navigated her car into town. "The Marine Corps was here before you and will be here well after you and your baby."

When she wasn't reminding me about my priorities as a mother-to-be, she was schooling me on the ways of an adult—the responsibilities I needed to keep in mind as I grew my family. She'd tell me things like, "Always keep money in your account for a rainy day," and "Get your will together; it's important that your family be protected," and "Think about your long-term goals. What do you see yourself doing in five years? How will you grow?"

She made me think and stretch in ways that I'd never considered, particularly as it related to raising children—particularly considering my family background and the trauma I'd experienced with my own birth mother. I was thinking bigger.

This was a small miracle in itself because I was pregnant in an era within the Marine Corps where mothers-to-be were not supported—when we were actively encouraged to seek conditional releases, which would allow a woman to list her pregnancy as a reason to get out of the military. I'd known quite a few women from boot camp who'd done this, citing that they wanted to focus their attention on a child rather than combat. Sergeant Douglas made me think differently.

"Your priority is to your child," she would add as I rubbed my growing belly. "Not to any man. Not to anyone else. But to your child. And don't let anybody make you feel bad about being pregnant."

That last point was particularly important, because had I been in the unit with the sergeant who chastised me for getting pregnant, surely I would have left the Marines. Giving up, though, wasn't an option for me, because the alternative—heading back to the destructive life I had in Chicago, this time with a baby on my hip—was what my nightmares were made of. Luckily, I found an advocate in people like Sergeant Douglas and Gunnery Sergeant Perez, both of whom ensured that I was focusing on bringing a healthy baby into the world regardless of what else was going on. Because of this, I was determined to be a better mother to my child than the one that I had been born to; giving up was not an option.

PREGNANT MARINES ARE EXEMPT FROM PHYSICAL TRAINING, but even as my baby grew and my body changed and my ankles got swollen, I made a point of participating—in part because I wanted to make sure I kept physically fit while pregnant, but mostly because I didn't want to send any messages that I couldn't handle carrying a baby in my belly and doing my job. I wanted my bounce-back after birth to be epically quick, specifically so that I could meet my weight standard and ace my first physical training test post-baby. So if my section was out running, I was out walking the trail with them.

This was not an easy proposition. I was still living in the barracks with roommates, I didn't have a car, and being pregnant limited my social interactions because, really, who was trying to hang out with a mom-to-be with a protruding belly? I still had to depend on my boyfriend for rides to work and back home and to doctors' appointments, and Sergeant Douglas continued to be a rock, inviting me over for dinner with her family.

In addition to trying to blend in as a pregnant woman on base, I was still dealing with a rough relationship with Carlo. We both tried harder to give each other grace while I was pregnant, because the way I saw it, this baby was a blessing—a chance to change the way a family structure looked on my watch. I knew I had what it took to raise my baby on my own, but that's not what I ultimately wanted; truly, I desired that picture-perfect traditional family, the "first comes love, then comes marriage, then comes baby in a baby carriage" kind of familial structure. I believed Carlo wanted that, too, as he was raised in a traditional family, with a mother and father in a happy home. He really stepped up to help me throughout my pregnancy, and eventually, he even proposed, saying it was important that we build together. When he asked me to marry him, he'd even gone so far as to ask my mom for her permission.

I told him no. Twice. No matter how much I wanted to create a traditional family, my gut told me that Carlo couldn't give me all of what I desired. Topping my list was loyalty—a committed relationship built on trust. Still, as my stomach grew and he stepped up to the plate, I slowly began to believe he would follow through on his promise to be the man I wanted—needed—him to be. So when he asked that third time, I said yes.

By April, we were married in a courthouse during a holiday pass; shortly after, I moved into an apartment with my new husband. By June, our baby, Destiny, was born. She arrived in the midst of extreme turmoil, with her father and I arguing and fighting, and me constantly questioning whether I'd made the right decision agreeing to wear this man's ring on my finger. When I stand back and look at the situation as a mother with more maturity, three marriages under my belt, and some wisdom under my wings, I can acknowledge that I was probably more concerned about creating this picture-perfect fantasy family than I was a space that would be healthy for both my baby and me, but at the time, I went along to get along.

What a mistake. Shortly after we married, I found out that

he'd been unfaithful. That intensified our arguing, which had already reached close to peak levels with the addition of the stress of caring for a newborn. Within months, our arguments got physical, culminating with him breaking my finger in the midst of an argument the night before Thanksgiving. I told the medic that a frozen turkey fell on my hand, but he knew better. Carlo spent that night in jail, and the two of us ended up at family services, taking classes to learn how to get along and raise our baby together. I hated that the medic eventually got the truth out of me, but what I hated even more was being so vulnerable—being in a position in which my husband could verbally, emotionally, mentally, and physically abuse me, the mother of his child. We were a rolling ball of dysfunction—everyone could see that—and before long, those who truly cared about me started asking the tough questions: "Why are you still with him?" "Why are you allowing him to do this to you?" "Why don't you make him leave?"

He spent the night in jail after breaking my finger, but he was right back home not too long after that. Then he got caught with marijuana and sentenced to thirty days in the brig—an aggressive punishment that was sure to lead to a dishonorable discharge. While he was gone, I got a taste of what it would be like to raise our daughter alone; it was tough but doable. I'd already worked to get my license and bought myself a car to get myself back and forth to work and to drive Destiny to day care, so I didn't have to depend on him for those things anymore. That part felt good.

But when he got out of the brig and awaited his discharge from the military, I did expect the man who'd said, "I do," with me, who helped me create our daughter's life, to step up to the plate and be the man and father I needed him to be. Instead, I got resistance and quite a bit of childish behavior. One morning, his actions even put my job in jeopardy.

I had to be at physical training at 0630, and I had every intention of being on time, most certainly because that's what time I was supposed to be there, but also because I didn't want anyone thinking I was using my baby as an excuse to be late. Thing is, Destiny's day care center didn't open until the same time I was supposed to be on base. I just knew that while I made my way to work, Carlo would be dropping the baby off at day care.

Boy, was I wrong. I was packing the baby's diaper bag when he started in. "I'm not taking her to day care. You got that."

"What are you talking about? I have to be at PT. You need to take the baby," I said through gritted teeth as I pulled on my uniform.

Soon enough, we were having a screaming match loud enough to make the baby cry. With an eye on the clock, I picked up my things, stormed out of the house, and tossed over my shoulder, "Take the baby to day care, man. That's all you have to do. You have one job here."

Rather than do that job, Carlo rushed out of the house with his keys, hopped into his own car, and chased my car down the street. There we were, practically drag racing through town, eyes red with fury, angry before the sun had even risen. And then, sheer terror set in. "Where is the baby?" I asked out loud.

So intent was Carlo on refusing to do what needed to be done for our daughter that he actually left the baby in the house. I was left holding the veritable baby bag, responsible for getting the baby to day care and getting to work, all at the same time.

Scared, angry, crying, and convinced my husband had lost his mind, I circled back home to collect my baby. Luckily, I wasn't quite yet out of our community, so I was able to race back and get Destiny. But rather than drop her off to day care and head to work late, I called my section and asked for the staff sergeant.

"I can't take it anymore!" I yelled, crying into the phone as I explained what had happened just moments earlier. "This is a disaster."

"You know what you have to do, right?" she asked.

"Yes," I said, sniffling. "I'm doing it now."

And with that, I hung up the receiver, dialed Carlo's unit, and got his gunnery sergeant on the phone. I repeated to him what I'd told my own supervisor: "He's got to go. I need someone to come to the house, get all his stuff, and remove him. I'm changing all the locks, and I want him gone."

Someone was at my house by early afternoon, standing over Carlo as he packed up his things and left our apartment.

Meanwhile, over at my unit, the entire office was celebrating. They had, after all, been telling me for months that I needed to get my stuff together and kick him out. If I had a nickel for every time they asked, "Why are you putting up with him?" I'd have been able to put in my papers and retire from the Marines a rich woman. But it took me a while to really listen to them—and especially to myself. I knew what we had wasn't working, but I kept trying to force it because I simply didn't want my child to be without a father, and I especially didn't want to be by myself in North Carolina, making a run as a single mom with no help from family. And with each transgression, I slowly got stronger and wiser: I took him to court. I called the cops when he got out of pocket. I secured a restraining order when I thought he would seriously hurt me. And finally I understood that trying to make our marriage work was causing more harm than it was worth. We were separated before our first anniversary, and he was gone from my life for good by our daughter's first birthday. Eventually, I took him to court for child support.

It took me some time, but I'd finally figured out for sure that the only person I could count on—that my child could count on—was me. I can't pretend that life was all sunshine and sunflowers when he was gone; being the sole caretaker for our daughter while being a full-time Marine was a struggle. But it was so much better than staying in that broken marriage.

Know this: walking away from a physically, mentally, emotionally, or financially abusive relationship isn't a sign of weakness. It is a power move—a show of pure strength.

I stayed with my ex for much longer than I should have because the lure of raising our daughter in a two-parent household was real for me, an adoptee who never truly realized the magic that comes from being raised in a stable, loving home by her birth parents. I'm not suggesting for one minute that I never witnessed a loving, stable, committed relationship up close; my adoptive parents were married for well over a quarter century before my adoptive dad died, and the two of them did work together to raise my siblings and me, plus take in countless other foster children in need of homes while their birth parents got themselves together. But I always thought there was something so much more special about that fairy-tale kind of family—the one that held tight to the traditional way of creating a most perfect, loving, smart partnership that would build a most perfect, loving, smart environment in which to raise the most perfect, loving, smart children.

But I learned the hard way after two trips down the wedding aisle that no relationship is a utopia, no partner is perfect, and no home is happy just because two people stood in front of a preacher, said, "I do," and slipped rings on each other's fingers. I also learned through my first marriage to Carlo, and my second husband, my daughter Jasmine's father, that I have every tool I need to be a warrior mom for my children, with or without a husband.

Now, it took me some time to get to this understanding. In my desperation to create this mythical, magical home for my daughters, I signed up to carry the weight for me, my babies, and men who didn't act as if they were as committed to creating the stable, loving family and home that I'd envisioned for all of us. One was abusive, the other just couldn't be what I needed him to be for me or my daughters, so I had to commit to moving forward on my own, ready, willing, and able to shake the deadweight so that I could lift up the kind of homelife my daughters and I needed.

I thought I'd found that in Donald, a fellow Marine who'd been my friend from our earliest days in the Marine Corps. We even played around with the idea of dating then, but lost touch and the opportunity to get together when he took a short leave of absence and came back, only to find that I was dating Carlo. Still, we kept in touch over all those years—through both marriages and my bouts as a single-mom Marine. Always, he showed concern for my well-being and that of my children, and he remained a good friend.

After losing touch for a few years, Donald popped up again, this time on Myspace. We started talking and reconnecting, and soon enough, that friendship, rock solid, turned into love, rock solid. What made him special was that he was able to match me toe-to-toe when it came to my attitude, which isn't easy. He was there for my daughters when their own fathers couldn't be the kind of dads the girls needed, and he supported me as I worked hard to create a stable life for our family.

But even that relationship was unsustainable. Despite our trying so hard to make it work, it just wouldn't. Couldn't. And we divorced, too.

Of late, I've been working on opening my heart and really examining what went wrong in my prior relationships, what role I played in their destruction, and figuring out what, precisely, I need in a mate to feel satisfied, loved, and whole. The only way I can figure that out, though, is by continuing to be brave—by stepping out on faith and trusting that I can handle doing what needs to be done to keep my daughters safe, housed, clothed, fed, and, above all else, loved. The more glass-is-full/do-what-makes-your-heart-beat-fast optimists among us would call this *choosing happy*.

Here are ways to be brave:

1. **Never, ever underestimate your own power.** You can do this. You can. But first you have to stop taking in other people's negative energy and naysaying and take control over how you

feel about yourself and your capabilities. Be firm but gentle with yourself and for God's sake, stop ceding control over your self-confidence to the whims of others. The opinions of your friends and family matter, sure, but they can't take precedence over how you feel about yourself and what you're capable of getting done. You have a purpose. You matter. And you can achieve whatever you prepare for and put in your mind to do, no matter what anyone else has to say about it. Make up your own mind, speak up for yourself, and go get what you want, confident in the fact that you have what it takes to complete that mission.

2.   Walk your own path. It's so easy to compare your own success to that of those around you, whether they're family, friends, or colleagues, and think that somehow you're a loser because you're not doing as well as they are. But every journey is as different as the people traveling it; each of us brings a different background, level of experience, talent, strength, and wisdom to everything that we do—variables that virtually guarantee that what we put into transitioning into something new, as well as the outcome, will be different from everyone else's. Applaud your friend for figuring out how to get free, and be open to her notes on how she made it to her current life station, but know that you have your own gut to follow, and it will steer you directly to where you need to be in its own time, on its own path, guided solely by what you packed in your own car.

3.   Remember: you started from the bottom, and now you're here. You've come a long way, baby. Know that. Stop harping on how hard it is to get to where you're going and how long it's taking you to get there, and focus on the analytics of this thing: your accomplishments mean something. They are chartable—they show your growth. When I think back to who I was as a teenager, wandering the streets with barely a plan for my life, hooking up with a crowd that loved me but was not good for me, I have to recognize that being a single mom, raising my first daughter without the help of her father, seemingly a million miles away from my family, with little help to feed, clothe, house, and protect her, was part of a huge upward trajectory for me. I was a good working mom. Still am.

4.   Don't worry about what others think. Friends, family—everyone will become specialists at telling you all the reasons why you can't step out on faith, why what you want to do won't work, why your dreams are nothing more than just that—dreams you can't accomplish in real life. What on earth do they know? Block out the negative talk—even the negative conversation you're having with yourself!—be optimistic and get to work.

This is what I want my children to know as they grow and watch and learn and set themselves on their own paths toward happiness. The most important lesson: being brave and choosing happiness requires hard work and commitment, first and foremost, and an understanding that happiness is a very fluid thing. It also requires you to stand steadfast in your own truth, no matter what others think about it. Sure, your mother may have a few things to say about you quitting your job—the one that pays you a decent wage, extends benefits to you and your family, and is as secure as a California redwood. Yes, you might get pushback from your friends who think it's better for you to stay in a marriage that's going nowhere because sticking to your vows takes precedence over personal happiness. But the armor you wear as a warrior helps you fight back the doubters and listen to your own voice as you bravely work toward the kind of joy *you* want for yourself. Honor that, and happiness will follow.

WARRIOR WORK

Chart your bravery. List ten ways you've used your courage in pursuit of happiness.

_____

_____

_____

_____

_____

_____

_____

_____

_____

_____

_____

_____

_____

_____

_____

_____

Make a list of ten happiness goals. What acts of bravery do you have to commit to fulfill those goals?

_____

_____

_____

_____

_____

_____

_____

_____

_____

_____

_____

_____

_____

_____

_____

Bravery is the engine of change.

—AISHA TYLER, COMEDIENNE, ACTRESS

8

WHATEVER IT TAKES: KNOW YOUR BIG REASON

THE WARRIOR CODE: PRINCIPLE #8

Love has reasons which reason cannot understand.

—BLAISE PASCAL, FRENCH MATHEMATICIAN, THEOLOGIAN

We can lean on a gang of things to help us achieve our goals: a trainer will help us get fit; a life coach will help us set personal and professional goals; going back to school will help us get that promotion we're looking for at work or gain the skills we need to switch careers altogether. But each of these goals only comes to fruition when you truly understand why you're doing them in the first place and put yourself in the proper mind-set to get the job done.

This is one of the first things we learn as Marines: our training, tactics, and equipment are vital, but it's our fighting spirit—our mind-set—that compels us to accept nothing less than victory. That mind-set makes us eager to fight and requires a high standard of excellence and a dogged determination to win, no matter what. I've taken that mind-set from the fields and used it with all that I've put my mind to: from, as a recruiter, convincing young people to consider the

Marines to, as the founder and lead organizer of my non-profit, Operation Heroes Connect, convincing troubled youth and veterans that they truly need one another to get whole. I've employed a "by any means necessary" mind-set to get my ultimate outcome, which is genuine connections between recruits and the service, and kids and veterans. The work, really, is the easy part. Keeping the right mind-set is what gets us through the challenges that threaten to derail the ultimate mission.

We've heard the saying before: success is 10 percent talent and 90 percent hard work. I'd venture to say that meeting goals involves the same percentages: success is 10 percent hard work, 90 percent mind-set. You have to know why you're doing something before you actually set about doing it, or you will fail every single time.

Think about it this way: you could get that gym membership on January 1 and say it's the first step to living up to your New Year's resolution to lose weight and be more active. But we all know how that story ends: by the beginning of February, each morning you're finding fifty more reasons for why you're going to skip working out: it's raining; you had a late night and need a little more sleep; the dog needs you; you can go another day (and that day never, ever comes). This happens because the mission—the "big reason"—was neither specific nor clear, just a part of the herd mentality of New Year's promises everyone makes and then breaks. But if you identify a real reason for getting in the gym (and it comes outside of some predetermined set of promises tied to the calendar), your ability to stick to it increases exponentially.

I've had a few big reasons for my greatest accomplishments,

chief among them my decision to go to the battlefield in time of war and my mission to make it back home alive. That first goal came in an instant on the morning of September 11, 2001, when America suffered an attack that was all at once shocking, infuriating—heartbreaking. I will never forget that morning: we sat there with our mouths open, eyes filled with tears, the silence in the room, save from the myriad of TVs blaring from practically every corner, thick and heavy. What was flashing before our eyes was unbelievable, unfathomable. But there it was, unfolding against the most picture-perfect, beautiful, clear blue sky: a jet plane careening through the air, aimed straight at the Pentagon. The casualties, we assumed, would be massive—the damage to this, the headquarters of the United States Department of Defense, incalculable. And that made what happened on September 11, 2001, personal for us Marines. It was as if someone deliberately, maliciously, dropped a bomb on our home, dead set on wiping out our parents, our sisters and brothers, our uncles and aunts. Family.

There wasn't a Marine in the room who wasn't ready to climb into our gear and head straight to the front lines. The call to duty, to defend our country and hold accountable whoever was responsible for this ungodly assault, was as palpable as our heartbeats—our very breaths. I was no exception. I wanted—needed—to get involved.

My chance would come in 2002 at the start of the Iraq War, while I worked at the GI headquarters. Though I was trained for combat, I was working in an administrative role. My job was to build from scratch the units needed for specific missions, establishing everything from who would be the commanding officer and sergeant major, down to how many infantry and artillery personnel and truck drivers would be in the units moving forward. This job also included submitting specific names for those missions, giving me the power to help decide which Marines would be sent overseas, including those who would be charged with fighting in the Iraq War. When I started creating those orders, I had my epiphany: I wanted to be among the number being sent into action. I told my boss just that.

"Not *no*, but *hell no*," he said emphatically.

"But I want to go," I insisted.

"Look, there's no way I'm letting you go to Iraq," he said firmly.

To understand why he was so against my going to Iraq, it's important to explain that my boss was a man's man—the kind who had certainly evolved to accept that women could serve in the military but who still had a hard time pulling the trigger on sending us into combat. In my case, that decision was all the harder because we were so close; we'd been working together for more than two years, and we'd become such good friends that we even threw baby showers for one another. He was invested in me. He was invested in all of us. Sending into the desert sands of Iraq a Marine whom he considered to be like a daughter to him, who also happened to be a single mom, was a no go. He knew the mission's stakes: it was the very beginning of a war in which we had yet to establish the power and reach of the enemy. It would be dangerous, and he didn't want me there.

I dropped the conversation with him, but that didn't extinguish my burning desire to do something—to rush in and fulfill my duty as a Marine to serve and protect our country. And the moment I saw an opening for an administrative chief in Iraq, I put my own name on the list to go out with an advance unit assisting in off-loading equipment and personnel, the most challenging of missions since there was no infrastructure yet established. In an advance unit, there are no tents set up, no living quarters, no bathrooms—nothing.

This is all to say that my supervisor's "hell no" didn't deter me. In fact, it made my desire to get my boots on the ground even stronger, much the way my brother's insistence that I wasn't fit for the Marines made me work harder to become one.

It took my boss, whose job was to look over and approve my suggestions for orders, a good week to notice I'd submitted my name. Angry, he called me into his office and ordered me to shut the door behind me.

"Why is your name on this manning document?" he asked, tapping his finger on the order I'd filled out.

"Sir, this is something that I really want to do. There is no reason why I can't go over," I said firmly, defending my decision. I wanted to go. I needed to go. I didn't want to be back in California, stuck in a support role, riding the bench while everybody else got to start. "I want to be out there, doing something for our country."

He let out a deep, heavy sigh and sat back in his chair. "What about your daughter? You have a child you're responsible for," he said.

"I can send my daughter to Chicago with my mom and family," I said simply. Little did he know, I'd already had a plan and readied an answer for every roadblock I knew he'd throw up to justify denying me the chance to serve in Iraq. For every excuse he had for why I shouldn't go, I had a justification for why I should. And in the end, I got my wish.

"Okay," he said finally. "Make sure you have your shit together. I don't want to hear anything about you changing your mind."

"You won't, sir. I got this."

I understood the risk: I was going to board a plane and fly overseas, directly into the fire, and to do that, I had to say goodbye to everyone I loved, knowing that I might never see them again.

Of course, I didn't explain it this way to my mother; there was no need. I kept the details of what I would be doing overseas to a minimum and made sure our conversation was simple and direct.

"Mom," I told her in a phone call, "I may be deployed soon."

"What will you do with Destiny?" she asked.

"She's going to have to come home to you."

"Okay," she said without hesitating.

It was as simple as that.

As I waited in California on standby for when we'd actually leave, I spent every precious moment I could with my daughter before I sent her to Chicago. When I got word that we would be leaving in November, I arranged for a friend, a fellow Marine, to take her back home. I'll never forget watching my daughter walk onto the plane with my friend, a see-through backpack full of Halloween candy bouncing on her little shoulders. Our tears could have filled an ocean.

Those emotions had played with me over the course of four

months. I know that sending her along when I did was the responsible thing to do, as being on standby meant that I could have as little as forty-eight hours to ship out. Still, I was lonely without my daughter, and it tore me to pieces that I missed cooking a special Thanksgiving meal for her and watching her open Christmas presents and kissing her cheek on the first day of the new year—milestone moments I'd spent with her along with every moment of her life.

This is the reality for a Marine: you have to be willing and ready to run directly toward the danger without hesitation, no matter the stakes. And my stakes were high: I had a daughter who, at the time, was only five years old—a baby. She needed her mother. But her mother needed to be a part of something bigger than even the two of us.

WHEN YOU'RE PACKING FOR DEPLOYMENT, you fill your bags with what is required and especially what is personally necessary to make it through six to nine months without the creature comforts of a cozy home. I had what would keep me physically alive—my 782 gear, which consisted of my uniforms, my Kevlar vest, boots, cold weather gear, poncho liners, pants, and all the other military-issue items the military requires of Marines ready to deploy. And then I had the things that would keep me emotionally alive: lots of pictures of my daughter; lots of DVD movies, Def Comedy Jam comedy shows, and music CDs, especially Ginuwine and Tupac, who was rapping in my ear when my feet hit the sand; and books, particularly the poetry of Maya Angelou. Rounding that out was an obscene amount of ramen noodles and my favorite snack, Flamin' Hot Cheetos, plus at least fifty pairs of underwear and enough baby wipes to supply a small day care center for months—necessities for marines who were marching into uncharted territory in a foreign land where there wasn't so much as a toilet, let alone a shower to get fresh and clean or a place to wash dirty panties.

Besides, there would be no time or room for niceties; we were headed into the desert in January as part of the Arrival and Assembly Operations Element (AAOE), the unit responsible for off-loading ships, tracking the accountability of personnel, and building camps. When we got into Iraq, it was so freaking cold! Standing in formation, at attention, under those circumstances was torture: we had to stand there and listen to the word while our hands froze and snot circles pulsed out of our noses. My hands went numb that first night; all I wanted to do was jump up and down and walk around to get my blood pumping through my veins, but instead, my body locked in place until I was able to shake it loose.

Shaking away the cold was nothing compared to shaking away the fear. The night of the American invasion of Iraq, I was part of the convoy that marched first across the desert sand. My position was A gunner, sitting up front on a seven-ton vehicle, driving through the pitch blackness—the eyes of our weapon. Our sole light source was the blasting rockets exploding and shimmying across the night sky, leaving a trail of light that signaled our reality: we were headed toward the danger. My heart raced as I considered the gravity of that and silently asked myself, *What the hell did you sign up for?* I was scared out of my mind, okay?

Still, there was no room for me to show that kind of weakness; I was a sergeant, and my driver was a lance corporal—two ranks below me. He had room to be shaky. I did not, especially in front of the Marines under my charge. Whatever I was feeling, I knew I had to bottle it all up and instead stick to keeping everyone calm, especially the younger Marines with barely any time under their belts, as we pushed forward through the thick of the darkness. I had to lead my men—keep them alert and focused. So I kept it as simple and straightforward as I could, asking, in an even tone, "You need water?" "You alert?" "You good?" I even asked the lance corporal random questions about his son, just to keep him engaged in conversation as we marched on for hours and hours. But deep inside, I was questioning my very existence: *Where the hell am I? What am I doing?*

Being surrounded by a long line of seven-ton trucks and my fellow Marines in front of and behind me made listening to the blasts and ricochet of the bullets bearable, for sure. There is solace in the numbers—the steady progression of the convoy, no one vehicle going faster than the other, advancing into the Iraqi darkness. The unknown. But when we were burying ourselves in fighting holes, near suffocating in our Mission Oriented Protective Posture (MOPP) suits, arms worn from holding position with our heavy weapons, bodies being whipped by sandstorms, the terror, for me, was agonizing. The flying sand, whipping against my skin like a million little switches working overtime to inflict pain on every bare surface of my body, made it impossible to see paces in front of us, which meant that we were constantly grappling with the unknown—if someone were standing right in front of us, ready to strike. Death was a real possibility.

In those moments, the one thing that kept me strong—that helped me make it out of those holes and those storms—was my daughter. I kept a picture of her in my headgear; every time I felt anxious or became racked with fear, I would look at her picture, see her sweet little face, and know that I was going to make it. Had to. For her sake. For mine. I knew, too, that being in harm's way was about assuring my daughter's safety for the future. Just like every other service member, I beat back my fear and longing with my reason: to make good on my commitment to protect and serve my country, certainly, but also to pave the way for a better future for my baby. Looking at that picture of her in day care, holding an umbrella, her toothy grin framed by a two thick pigtails on either side of her moon-pie face, consistently reminded me of my reason: dying was not an option because I had to get back to my child.

My big reasons for going to war and making a point of getting back home were as crystal clear as my reasons for being in Iraq were passionate: I wanted to actively fight for my country and come back home to my daughter. My *whys* for going and coming back were simple, focused, clear, and profound, and identifying it up front got me into the right frame of mind to pack my bags, get on that plane, and step out into the unknown, confident that I would accomplish my two ultimate goals. My goals, then, were my drivers—my motivation. If I had neither of those, I'd have stayed in California, creating orders for my fellow Marines and going home to my child, overrun with angst and the nagging feeling that I wasn't doing my part. Staying home wasn't an option. And neither was dying. My whys propelled me.

To find your big reason for making moves, first you have to ask yourself the hard questions: Are you doing it for the approval of others? Are you doing it because someone else said you should? Are you following the crowd? Or are you genuinely doing this because of the love of it? Will you be better off because of it?

Honest answers to these questions will lead you directly to your big reason, which gives you the definitive answer for why you're doing what you're doing in the first place, and attach purpose, desire, and passion to your mission so that you can actually see it through. Here's how you find your big reason and honor it:

1. Set the goal. Do this with intention and be really specific about what you're going to do and why you're doing it. Don't bother making weak declarations—"One of these days, I'm going to travel the world" is nothing but a vague wish any twelve-year-old can say out loud, fully knowing he's just talking to hear his own voice. Define exactly what you plan to do: "Next summer, I'm going to visit China, and the summer after that, I will go to Cuba, because I want to travel the world." These are perfectly attainable goals with precise dates to help hold you accountable. Push this out even further: plan the entire trip—where you'll stay, what you'll do when you get there, how you'll travel both to the country and within it, too, down to the two fancy restaurants at which you plan to eat on two special nights—and keep those plans in a special folder with a picture of the country on the top. Drop that bad boy on your desk or nightstand and you'll have set your goals with intention. It's the perfect first step to making them come to fruition.

2.   See the big reason. Don't just say it out loud; get yourself a physical representation of what you're trying to achieve. For me, my goal of getting back home was represented by my daughter's picture; seeing her face was a constant reminder that I needed to do whatever it took to not only complete my mission but also do it in a way that would secure my safety so that I could see her in person again and get back to doing what I do best: being a good mother to my child. Perhaps your goal is to ace a test that will give you the license you need to start your own business. If your big reason for taking that test is to get your business off the ground, get yourself some business cards with the name of your company in bold, raised, fancy letters, put them in a card holder, and place them somewhere where you can see them every day. Put one in your wallet, too, so that every time you go to buy something, you're reminded to take it easy with the spending because you're in the midst of building an empire.

3.   Be ready to pay—in sweat. Nobody said seeing your goal through would be easy. It'll take talent to achieve your goal, sure, but it'll also take hard work. You won't just be able to walk into the gym and, after a couple of weeks of working out with the trainer, miraculously be thirty pounds lighter with a body that'll be paparazzi ready. You're going to be sore. Your body is going to be asking you, "What in the hell?" You're going to want to give up. And chances are that with all that hard work and dropping that thirty pounds, you won't look like Kim Kardashian by the time you reach your weight loss goal. Push on anyway with your big reason at the forefront of your mind, mindful that complacency is your enemy. Looking to make that move to a new job with the better title, higher salary, and super perks? Put in the work and build your muscle:

get that LinkedIn profile together; read up on the people who've held the position, and chart their successes and mistakes so that you can learn from them; take that class that'll help you perfect a skill you'll need to bring with you to the new position. If you want to soar, you're going to have to be really deliberate about teaching yourself how to fly the highest, hardest, and furthest. It may be tough, and in some cases, it may not be all that enjoyable, but this is the price you'll pay to realize your goals.

4. Let your haters be your motivators. Be clear: I'm not saying you should give any kind of damn about the thoughts and wishes of someone who wants to see you fail. They don't deserve that kind of power over your goals or your big reason. But when you're having that day when you're full of doubt, you're tired, you're dragging, you're not feeling encouraged, there's nothing like a hater to make you pick your step back up. See, the haters are sitting around rubbing their hands together, just watching and waiting for you bow out, pick up your ball, and go on home. Why give them the satisfaction? Why let their hate distract you from getting the job done? Instead, use them to inspire yourself to higher heights. That old boss who said you were incapable of doing that job you were hoping you would be promoted to but didn't get? Imagine how wide you'll smile when you shake his hand and reintroduce yourself using that new title of yours. Turn him into one of your big reasons, and then play to win, even and especially when you're close to running out of steam.

5. Use that temporary goal to fuel a lifelong goal. Here's the thing: had I stayed behind that desk in California when the United States headed to Iraq, I would have missed out on a lot of blessings. Being in the field, serving as the advance team charged with securing and setting up units ready to complete their missions opened doors for me; had I not been there, maybe I wouldn't have been motivated to start my own nonprofit. Had I not started my own nonprofit, maybe I wouldn't have caught the attention of those television producers, looking for me to represent the Marines in *American Grit*. I probably wouldn't be writing this book, either, if it weren't for that show. My point is that I changed who I was and committed myself to something I'd never done before with the temporary goal of fighting for my country in a war that I knew eventually would end, and that choice changed me in ways that allowed me to do a myriad of things I wouldn't have dreamed of doing. You don't necessarily see what the lifelong goal is until you pursue that temporary goal right in front of your face, and it opens the door to new possibilities. Infinite possibilities.

WARRIOR WORK

What are the three big reasons that get you out of bed in the morning? List them and all the ways they inspire you to set and attain your goals.

List three big goals you plan to accomplish over the next twelve months. List the big reasons that will help you achieve those goals.

_____

_____

_____

_____

_____

_____

_____

_____

_____

_____

_____

_____

_____

_____

_____

It must be borne in mind that the tragedy of life doesn't lie in not reaching your goal. The tragedy lies in having no goals to reach.

—BENJAMIN E. MAYS, EDUCATOR AND ACTIVIST

9

GUNG-HO (WORK TOGETHER): FIND YOUR TRIBE

THE WARRIOR CODE: PRINCIPLE #9

> *Sometimes being a friend means mastering the art of timing. There is a time for silence. A time to let go and allow people to hurl themselves into their own destiny. And a time to prepare to pick up the pieces when it's all over.*

> *—GLORIA NAYLOR, AUTHOR*

Next to family and an intimate relationship with God, there is nothing more beautiful, more spiritual, more important than a squad of friends. The good friends, the buddies we choose and with whom we solidify relationships built to last, are the ones you can laugh with and lean on—the ones who motivate you, believe in you, tell you about yourself, or simply provide a shoulder when you need support or comfort. They're the ones you can count on. When we make that magical connection with other human beings, they pack a wallop in good vibes, amazing experiences, and a firm focus on what truly matters. We make one another happy.

These are not easy relationships to come by or keep. When we're kids, we're friends with any ol' body, made easy by proximity: if children are in the same school class, climbing the same jungle gym at the park, running down the same soccer field chasing the ball toward the goal, voilà, they're friends. Connecting with like-minded people as young adults can be equally effortless: hit up a party, put in work at the gym, partner up in a study group to ace that college physics test and the camaraderie practically falls in your lap. Some of those friendships stand the test of time, sure, but they morph with life changes: someone moves, or graduates, or falls in love and builds a family and an intimate relationship of his or her own, and friendships can fade with the physical and emotional distance that accompanies that evolution. Responsibilities kick in and, after a while, the childhood and young adult friendships we thought would last forever become commemorative—friendships we remember fondly but that we've actively sidelined for relationships that take precedence: spouses, children, our jobs, family members who need our attention.

And that's when adult friendships come in—the ones that may take some time and considerable effort to make but that can come with rock-solid bonds that nestle in the heart. Those are the ones that make life sweet—even and especially when it's overrun with very grown-up responsibilities. They fulfill our needs—psychological, emotional, physical—in a way that makes us feel heart-to-heart, soul-to-soul connected.

When I was in active duty, I had a band of brothers who looked out for me from jump: no questions, no hesitation. It could have been easy for them to turn their backs on me. After all, I was one of the first women with one of the first units to land in Kuwait to prepare for the invasion of Iraq and the only female in my section of forty Marines. I didn't plan it like this; when I put my name on the ticket to be the admin chief in that particular unit headed for Iraq, I bargained and maneuvered and did what I needed to do to get the job. Never once did it occur to me to check over the list of names to see what genders, races, or cultural backgrounds from which my fellow Marines hailed.

The divide got real, though, once we got boots on the ground and had to figure out the logistics of living together. There would be more than two dozen Marines sleeping together—all men, except me. I saw the two gunnery sergeants responsible for setting up sleeping arrangements standing up front, looking perplexed and talking in hushed tones. "But where is she going to sleep?" one asked as they both shifted their eyes in my direction. Finally, one posed the question outright: "Sergeant Evans, you have two choices: you can either sleep in a tent by yourself down the way," he said, pointing his finger into the darkness, past the area where our unit intended to set up its sleeping quarters, "or you can sleep in here with the men. What's it gonna be?"

It was in that moment—and that moment only—that I felt like an individual who didn't fit in, rather than a part of the whole.

"What do you all think? Are you okay with her being in here with the guys?" the gunnery sergeant continued without giving me a chance to answer the original question.

The yeses, thank goodness, were emphatic. Not one man objected to my being in the tent with them.

The gunny slowly scanned the room to make sure there were no objections, then turned his eyes toward me. "Evans? You good with that?"

"Yes, Gunny, I'm good," I said quickly. "I would rather be here than out somewhere by myself."

And that was that.

Now, though the decision was easily made with zero push-back, I couldn't help but feel somewhat awkward; it would be, after all, one female and more than three dozen men in my tent, our cots perfectly aligned one after the other, four feet apart. We would be closer than close at all times. I didn't have the luxury of having other women to talk to or women's-only bathing areas and bathrooms. If I had to use the bathroom, I dug a ditch. If I was hungry, I ate what I had or what was available to everyone else for free, courtesy of the Marines. If I got my period, I handled it. There was no stopping what I was doing because it was that time of the month or I had cramps or anything like that. We needed to move of one accord; there was no time for delicateness.

I did wonder whether they would resent me because they'd have to get dressed somewhere separately, knowing a woman was living in their sleeping quarters, or if they'd change the way they talked among one another because they needed to watch their language in front of a female. I thought, too, about what kind of treatment I'd face as a woman—whether any of the men would say sexist things to me or, worse, assault me because I was the only female in sight. But there was none of that. Not even a little bit. In fact, each of my fellow Marines treated me like a sister, and I looked at them as my brothers because that is what we are out there—family. United. Never once did I hear anyone utter, "Oh, what's she gonna do? She's a female." I'm a smart-mouthed, tall, strong Chicago girl; they knew I could hold my own. And they went out of their way to make me comfortable. My brothers made me a makeshift dresser out of wood and cardboard to keep my things in, and one put his cot between the door and mine so that I wouldn't have to sleep directly next to the tent's entrance. We even had a little makeshift dinner table we'd sit at while eating our MREs or whatever food we brought from back home. It wasn't the level of what one would get in a hotel—not by a stretch—but it was what we came to know as home. For me, it was perfect.

Their benevolence got me through, especially when it came to human connection. I was really cool with the communications guys—the techies of the bunch, who always had the coolest movies, the latest games, and total control over the phones. They came prepared. If your computer was down and you got that blue screen of death while you were out there in the desert, they were the ones who would quickly come and fix your entire technological life. So it was good to be buddies with them.

This was especially so after our first mission ended, and we moved forward into the heart of Iraq, where we'd spend the next few months with the Force Service Support Group, working at the Combat Operations Center. This was the hub of our operations, where many of the intelligence, personnel, ammo, and security briefings for the general took place. It was there that one of the comm guys was especially kind to me. Knowing that I was a single mom and that I had a daughter back in Chicago, he arranged it so that I could talk to my baby and family whenever I wanted. This was a miracle on the order of Jesus turning water into wine because the only time we could communicate with our families via phone was during "morale calls," a highly emotional three-minute phone call we were allowed to make only on occasion. The first few I'd made back home tore me to pieces; hearing my baby's voice, only to have to rush her off the phone in the middle of a story about her day or a new friend or some big accomplishment in school, felt like a shank to my lung. I could barely breathe by the time I'd hang up.

That I worked overnight from midnight to noon the next day helped with my ability to communicate with my family and friends back home; I deliberately signed up for the shift knowing that it would allow me to email my family at a time when they'd be awake and able to answer me back relatively quickly. But my friend in the comm department went the extra mile by actually hooking me up with my own phone line. He literally ran an extra-long wire under the sand from the comm tent to my cot in my own tent, where I had my very own tact line. Now, a *tact line* is a phone that can call military numbers only, but I had the hookup back at my shop in California; my former supervisor advised everyone there to patch me through to my family in Chicago whenever I called. They'd turn the call into a three-way, put the phone down, and let me talk for as long as I liked.

My Marines back in California sent a gift to me in Iraq that I completely didn't expect; I hadn't received much of anything from anyone while I was out there, but there was this box, shipped all the way from California, with my name carefully written in neat block letters. I practically giggled while I ripped it open. I reached in and pulled out . . . a bottle of mouthwash, wrapped with what had to be at least a half roll of duct tape.

I crinkled my nose and held the bottle up to the light. "Mouthwash?" I said to no one in particular.

As I cut through the duct tape, it hit me: what was in the

bottle wasn't mouthwash at all. It was a fine bit of liquid spirits to lift my spirits out there in the middle of that desert. What's more, it was the perfect gift to share and connect with the Marines I was bonding with in Iraq.

Now that I'm older, I can appreciate all those things I took for granted at the time; I never asked for any of it—the dresser, the cot positioning, the phone line, the liquor, the respect of every last one of the sixty men in my unit. They cared about my well-being and looked out for me in ways that they simply didn't have to. They made me a priority. For that, I'm grateful.

I did have a few mishaps that may have been exacerbated by the fact that I'm a woman. Like the time when we were setting up our base camp and I peed myself because I couldn't get my MOPP gear off quickly enough after running to the Porta-John. I gather that if you're a guy, you can unsnap, unzip, and unbutton a few strategic places rather quickly to get the access a man would need to urinate. But we women need to work our way through all those snaps, zippers, and flaps; pull down the gear; then take off our uniform pants and wind through a few more layers before we can actually sit down and do what we need to do. I'd been holding my pee for hours while building and fixing up our little tent, as I didn't want to leave my responsibilities to anyone else. But by the time we'd finished, I'd been holding on for so long that I just couldn't hold it long enough to disrobe. Female problem.

Then there was another bathroom break that landed me, literally, in a pile of shit. I made a point of waiting until nighttime to handle bathroom business that required complete privacy, and on this particular night, I headed out into the pitch-black dark to get to our makeshift toilet, which consisted of a paint can with a few strategically placed pieces of wood to make up the toilet, and a crude assembly of more wood to create a stall. We couldn't use a flashlight to guide our steps at night because it could potentially give away our position, so we had to learn rather quickly how to navigate the desert to get to it under the cover of darkness, with only the light of the moon to make out silhouettes of landmarks. I was headed in the right direction, but just two kilometers to the left was the burn pit—a ditch in which we emptied the paint can and then burned the contents to keep our camp sanitary—which I miscalculated on my walking path. I went in one moment from walking to falling directly into the burn pit. I mean, I just literally dropped straight in.

As disgusting as it was to be buried to my waist in excrement, I didn't scream out because I didn't want to awaken my fellow Marines, or disturb whoever was on watch, or, worst of all, alert any enemies to my position. Besides, there'd be no helping me out of this one: I had to figure out how to get myself out of the pit and climb out of my MOPP without letting any of the urine or feces touch my hands.

Somehow, I managed to get out of my MOPP suit, and then I used my e-tool, a digging utensil, to bury it deep in the ground. Then I scrubbed myself near raw with baby wipes so that no one could detect the stench that seemed like it was pouring from every pore. By the time I made it back to camp, I smelled like a newborn. That's how much I scrubbed. There was no way I was going to go back to the camp and tell any of my brothers I fell in the burn pit. I planned to take that story to the grave. Waiting to move one's bowels until after all the men were sleeping? Another female issue, for sure.

Other than those instances, though, our differences never really mattered; I had so many other things running through my head, the fact that I was the only female was the least of my worries. This was my first time deploying, and because we had no operation procedures in place, we were making up everything as we went along. We knew we had to have each other's backs or we wouldn't survive. There was no male or female, no black or white, no Southerner or Northerner—there were only Marines out there.

Not everyone can have the bond that my brothers and I built with one another in the sands of Iraq. But friendships are most necessary for a warrior's total well-being. Here's how you find the lifelong adult friendships that keep you sane, in check, happy, supported, and loved:

FIRST, CHECK YOUR FRIENDSHIP INVENTORY. No one human being can be everything to you, so you'll need a collection of friends who can serve a variety of needs that will make your interpersonal relationships whole. Assess what you need in a true friendship: Is it someone who listens? Someone who gives great advice? Someone who encourages you to find peace and joy? Someone who implores you to take care of yourself? Or maybe someone who will ride shotgun with you while you explore your wild side—that one who'll be sitting on the jail bench high-fiving you and saying, "But damn, that was fun!" Once you figure out what you need in a friend, take stock of who in your circle provides one or more of those things for you, and then pour into each one according to what they bring to the table. For example, if one of your friends is forever pouring into you the need to take better care of your body, why not partner with her to go to a weekly yoga class or join together to do a "no sugar or carbs" eating challenge? You'll bond over the shared goal, thus solidifying your connection. Bonus: you'll get a return on your investment by getting into better shape and eating more healthily. Score!

FIGURE OUT WHO IS WORTHY of being in your circle of trust. Be clear: not every person who is friendly to you is a friend. You save that title for the people who, when hard times hit, will be able to be counted on to be there for you when you need them most. Being there means they'll lend their shoulder, ear, advice, car keys—whatever—without hesitation or judgment, no matter how good or bad the actions that got you stuck. Trust, when something bad goes down and you're at your lowest, the angels among your friends will reveal themselves. Those are the keepers. That's your squad.

IF YOU WANT GOOD FRIENDS, you have to be a good friend. It's that simple. It's unreasonable and most certainly unfair to demand someone's undivided attention and loyalty and do nothing to return the favor. The same ones who help you be a better you are the ones who deserve your unconditional, nonjudgmental support. Say one of your friends is going through it with her husband and she's confided in you that her relationship is on the rocks: a good friend would offer to take the kids off her hands for a few hours or even for a sleepover with "Auntie" so that she can have some time alone to plan her next move or spend some quality grown-up time working out the problem with her spouse. Or maybe you're the one who ponies up for a spa day for you and your bestie after she's told you about a disastrous week at work that's nearly broken her. Whatever your strong suit is, pour it into the friends who love and care for you. That's what friends do.

BECOME YOUR OWN BEST FRIEND. Of course, it's important to have a squad that's got your back, but really, who's going to fend for you harder than you? Who's going to want the best for you more than you? Who's going to treat you better than you? It's high time you poured into yourself the way you do others, with passion and intent. Exercise. Take a walk in the park, rocking out to your favorite playlist as you take in that good vitamin D straight from the sun and breathe in that fresh air. Go to the museum and then out to lunch by yourself, filling yourself with good food for your soul and your belly. See a therapist to help you process your own issues and figure out ways to get out of your own way. Think about what makes you happy and then go do it; get full on the joy you put on your own plate. Pursuing our own passions, on our own terms, for ourselves, builds up character and confidence and sets us up to be the kind of friends our friends need us to be to them.

MAKE YOUR MOVE. Look, the days of knocking on the new neighbors' door and asking the new kid to come out and play are over; that kind of magical connection just doesn't happen often for adults who are busy, well, adulting. If you want to make someone's acquaintance, and you'd genuinely like that acquaintance to bloom into a full-blown friendship, you're going to have to put yourself out there and create the opportunities for you all to bond. Maybe the coworker you've really connected with at work is a reader: invite her to read and talk about a book over coffee, like your own private book club. Have a group of guys you're interested in getting to know better? Invite them over to watch the game and have a few beers. Organize a group mani/pedi trip at that new nail salon with the fancy stations and free champagne. Or put together a themed movie night in your basement, replete with all Morris Chestnut's best movies and lots of freshly popped popcorn. Bonus: tell each friend to bring a friend so that everyone gets to meet new people to add to their circle. Whatever it is, plan it and the people will come, giving you a more intimate setting ripe for deepening friendships.

MAKE THE TIME. Life gets hectic when you're trying to be a good husband and you're working that extra shift to get in that overtime cash and you're shuttling the kids back and forth to soccer practice and every day starts melting into the next and time keeps on slipping away. Sometimes that means your good friends fall way on down the list of priorities. Make them priorities by scheduling check-ins. No, literally schedule them in. Put it in your calendar, write it in your phone, time it with something that happens routinely, like a trip to the barbershop every two weeks: at that specific time, you will hit them up on their cell, send a text, or email them an update on what's happening in your life and asking them about their own. This helps you stay connected and creates more opportunities for you to plan in-person catch-ups that wouldn't normally happen if you weren't checking in. You could also go beyond a verbal check-in and get bigger: schedule a bi-weekly dinner or a monthly trip to a sporting event or a quarterly hiking trip. Whatever it is, it'll keep you both in each other's space, even when everyday life takes up the majority of your time, space, and brain matter.

KICK NOT-SO-FRIENDLY FRIENDS TO THE CURB. Seriously, who has time for toxic friendships? If she's gossipy, emotionally draining, mentally exhausting, and downright destructive when it comes to herself or your relationship, why be bothered? Do what you can to make the relationship work if she's worth the trouble, but if you just don't see any redeeming qualities and the friendship is actively hurting you, and your heart is telling you, "Listen, you're wasting your time," follow your gut and toss it. You're grown. You are not obligated to hold on. You get what you allow. Don't allow it. Don't look back. Just go.

Build that squad and you've got something special on your hands—a group of people who are genuinely emotionally, mentally, spiritually, physically on your side, actively working to make your brain, heart, and gut that much stronger.

WARRIOR WORK

Write the names of your closest friends and the relationship role each plays in your life.

Document the ways you've been a good friend to them.

List the ways you can be a better friend to your friends.

_____

_____

_____

_____

_____

_____

_____

_____

_____

_____

_____

_____

List ten ways you can meet new potential friends.

_____

_____

_____

_____

_____

_____

In everyone's life, at some time, our inner fire goes out. It is then burst into flame by an encounter with another human being. We should all be thankful for those people who rekindle the inner spirit.

—ALBERT SCHWEITZER, FRENCH-GERMAN THEOLOGIAN

10

READY FOR ALL, YIELDING TO NONE: STAND YOUR GROUND

THE WARRIOR CODE: PRINCIPLE #10

> *I prefer men who don't fall down and weep, who absorb a blow, who do not scamper and yell when chased, but stand firm, crouch, square off, meet an attack with something like resistance, even if it kills them.*

> *—BEN MARCUS, AUTHOR*

It wasn't until the advent of social media, really, that people started truly expressing themselves. But speaking your mind in 140 characters on Twitter, or on a private Facebook page post to your twenty cousins and a stray friend or two, or in a comments section where people tend to say the most disgusting things under the guise of anonymity simply isn't the same thing as speaking your truth with authority and conviction in real life.

The truth is, we're a country that's long demanded people bottle up their feelings and keep their opinions to themselves. This isn't just a Marine thing; this is a human condition— even here in America, the land of the free. For all that we say about loving the First Amendment, we Americans are terrible about encouraging each other to speak freely and from the heart. In fact, we've long actively discouraged it, dismissing opinions and expression as impolite. It starts from when we're kids; parents insist that children be seen and not heard, or they demand that kids be "nice" and fine-tune the art of being a people pleaser by saying what others want to hear, rather than what they truly mean, so as not to offend or come off as arrogant. This follows us into adulthood, where we're constantly screaming our opinions and feelings in our own heads but self-editing before the words escape our mouths so as not to offend or change people's perceptions of us.

What this leads to is a nation of people talking into our own silos online and, in person, tempering—if not altogether skipping—conversations about money, politics, sex, and race. We play nice in mixed company, playing ourselves small and allowing others to get away with behavior that is hurtful at best and that renders us powerless at worst.

Warriors stand tall in their convictions, no matter what. With no matter who. Anywhere, anytime. No matter how hard.

I had to do this with my own family. Like many military families with loved ones serving overseas, my mom had a yellow ribbon wrapped around a tree towering out in front of our apartment building back in Chicago and my official Marine Corps graduation photo in the front window, a testament to her unyielding support for me while I was serving in Iraq. It was an incredibly sweet, heartfelt gesture; it felt good to know that my family was making a very public statement about the military, my dedication to fighting for our country, and, most importantly, my deployment to Iraq, even as a growing sector of civilians was being highly critical of then president George W. Bush's decision to wage war after the terrorist attacks on September 11, 2001.

But then, during a short call home, I learned rather quickly during a conversation with my daughter, then only five years old, how my family really felt about my deployment.

"Mommy, you're still at war because that mean man Bush sent you to get his oil," she said, her sweet voice bouncing in my ear, making my heart race.

I was livid. I mean, I knew the sentiment came from a place of love, and I understood the words and the whys: I'm African American, from a black community and a staunchly black family—neither of which truly believed in or supported Operation Iraqi Freedom and both of which feel some kind of way about black people serving in the military and possibly dying while defending a country with a history of turning its back on our community. What's more, my family didn't know that I'd submitted my own name and actively campaigned to go to Iraq, despite that my immediate supervisor was against me going, and so they were operating under the assumption that I was swept up into the legions of soldiers fighting a war that, in their minds, we shouldn't have been fighting. Coming clean on that front would have had them looking at me like I was totally crazy—like I'd lost my mind supporting "that white man's war."

Still, my daughter's words angered me for several reasons: I knew that she was simply repeating very grown-up conversations she had no business hearing in the first place; engaging in rhetoric about Bush being evil and allegedly hating black people flew directly in the face of my duty as a Marine to respect my commander in chief, no matter who he or she was; and such declarations completely dismissed my feelings of patriotic duty to go overseas to fight for my country, rather than to sit in an office sending other people's sons and daughters and husbands and wives to do the fighting for me.

This is what we consistently face when we choose to wear the uniform, though: the entire world, it seems, has something to say about our choice to serve, even as we are forced to couch our own opinions while we serve. To some, we are strong and brave and righteous, worthy of applause; to others, we are robotic killing machines, too dumb and blindly patriotic to understand or care about the nuance of war; to even more, we are conservative bullies excited to put our muscle into bending the world to the will of America.

Here's my truth: I am Tawanda Marie Hanible from Chicago. I am a Marine. I am a mother. I am a daughter. I am a friend. I am passionate and interesting, smart and opinionated. I believe in my country, but I don't blindly follow behind anyone's political opinions or social beliefs. I am a black woman in America who identifies as a Democrat, but I support our right to bear arms and own a gun. Just as I believe in defending my country, I believe in protecting my family. I am military, but I refuse to blindly support the police, especially when the conversation turns to police brutality and its effects on the black community. I believe in a woman's right to plan her own parenthood. I am a feminist. I am a human being with layered thoughts and beliefs that don't have to line up with everyone else's thinking in order for me to embrace them. And when I believe in something—truly feel it deep down in my gut—arguing with me about it won't change my mind, because I am opinionated and strong willed, too. I was born this way.

Understand, it was no easy proposition for an opinionated character like me to be in the military. I had a voice for seventeen years before I joined the military, and as soon as I got in, like each of my fellow Marines, I had to button my lips, check my emotions, and keep my opinions to myself. It was policy—an institutional mandate. But it was also a rank-and-file directive that made life in the office quite a challenge, to say the least. Every moment of the day, from sunup to sundown, everybody and their mama could tell us what to do, particularly if we were young and fell low on the rank structure. The higher the rank you picked up, the fewer people there were correcting you and telling you what you should and shouldn't do, but institutionally, if we were wearing a uniform, we were rendered mute. As a service member with morals and beliefs, all too often you find yourself having to mute your beliefs and instead follow orders that sometimes contradict those beliefs. Watching children being detained on your base and kept away from their families is definitely an example of having to mute your beliefs.

Dealing with this was tough in my formative years in the Marines, but it wasn't until around the last five years that it really became a problem for me. The difficulties came around 2011, just as I started getting recognized for my work as a woman in the Marines as well as the head of Operation Heroes Connect. As awards started flowing in, interview requests peaked, and every time a news outlet asked to speak to me, I would have to go through a long debriefing on what I could and couldn't say, what uniform I could and couldn't wear, who I could and couldn't talk to. It became so frustrating that after a while, I didn't want to do them anymore; the restrictions were hampering my ability to speak even positively about all the great things that were happening with my charity, or even details about my personal life that I was willing to share.

What's worse is that this was all happening just as social media began to explode with movements highlighting hot-button political and social issues, like the high-profile police shootings of unarmed African Americans on video, legislation aimed at turning back the clock on reproductive rights, discourse on poverty, the school-to-prison pipeline, and the housing crisis. I had plenty to say about it all, but neutrality was the order of the day, which rendered me voiceless on issues that I wanted desperately to speak about—loudly.

A major breaking point for me was when the Charleston church shooting occurred. On that fateful day, a lone man joined a Bible study group at Emanuel African Methodist Episcopal Church, and, after praying with them, opened fire, killing nine parishioners. The killer and avowed racist admitted he killed black people specifically to start a race war, a declaration that eventually led prosecutors to charge him with a hate crime and call him a terrorist. Still, the morning after the shooting, while waiting with my superiors to start a conference call with the battalion, the commanding officer fixed his mouth to blame the parishioners for their own deaths. "See, that's what they get for not having guns," he said nonchalantly, leaning back in his chair. My anger was palpable; his comment made me so hot, I'm sure that if he looked close enough, he could have seen heat waves rising from my head. I was so pissed I had to excuse myself.

There were so many instances where I found myself in an audience of higher-ups whose viewpoints were simply not the same as mine, and because I was a lower rank, I had to sit and listen without commentary. By my final year, I literally had to give myself pep talks just to get out of my car and walk into work—that's how frustrated I was. My only relief was knowing that eventually, I'd get away from those toxic people; either my time serving at that particular station would end or that person would transition out of the office and rotate to a new station.

But getting out of a station didn't change the overall culture of the corps or how some of my fellow Marines dealt with me as a woman and a rising star within the ranks. Getting invited to the White House and profiled in *Newsweek* was meant to shine a bright spotlight on the Marine Corps, and it did that, sure. But that spotlight also shone a harsh glare on me, putting a target on my back and enticing fellow Marines to ask, "What makes her so special? Why her?" The people who were supposed to be mentors were, perhaps, the harshest of all, particularly when I received kudos from higher-ups. One evening after a commanding general congratulated me for planning, sponsoring, and hosting a Thanksgiving dinner for homeless veterans, a female major whom I looked up to actually questioned how I found the time to put in the work I was doing for my nonprofit and the various charitable events I'd successfully completed.

"I mean, aren't you a mom? Why are you doing all of this?" she sniffed. "I hope you weren't doing any of that during working hours."

Of course, I hadn't done any work while on the job; I was staying up until 2:00 A.M. making sure we had all that we needed to feed the people—a job for which I should have been proud. But her words stung—depleted me, taking me from the high of being praised to the low of feeling like I was being ridiculed for wanting to lend a helping hand. Interactions like that—and my inability to clap back at such disrespect and malcontent—contributed to my love/hate relationship with the Marine Corps. It was as if someone had ordered me to sit in a corner and shut up and color for two decades, blissfully ignorant to what was going on around us and afraid to take any kind of initiative or leadership outside of what was right in front of us.

That kind of treatment was only heightened by the fact that I am a woman in the Marines. Though I am lauded for being one of the first to be allowed into combat and I've made lifelong companions of male Marines with whom I've worked over the years, being a woman in the Marine Corps was no cakewalk. When it comes to gender and racial diversity, truly I believe we have the furthest to go as far as making real change, and this observation is only heightened when one is a black woman. Every ounce of hate I've ever gotten as a Marine has come from "brothers" who I feel have been conditioned by this male-dominated institution to disregard and display a level of hate toward female marines that stretches far beyond "jokes." It's actually instilled in young recruits, who are regularly told that females are dirty and disgusting and untouchable when it comes to forming romantic relationships because we're "not worth it." This is the kind of training that leads to incredibly sexist behavior among the ranks. Take, for instance, the explosive scandal in which members of Marines United, a private Facebook page for Marines and veterans, got caught posting thousands of pictures of female Marines either nude or engaged in sexual acts, without the women's consent. The posts were accompanied by all kinds of lewd remarks about their bodies, plus outrageously violent commentary on ways these men wanted to hurt the very women they're supposed to regard as "sisters." The page eventually was shut down, the Marine Corps and NCIS launched investigations, and a Marine spokesman released a statement threatening various charges against any Marine found to be involved, but not even a month after the page was shut down, another popped up in its place, with even more pictures and lewd comments, plus taunts and threats for both whistleblowers and investigators who were working to expose those in the second secret group.

Female Marines were incensed, scared, but we all knew in our heart of hearts that nothing would come of it. Sure, the media blowback was fierce and the threats flew—even Congress threatened to get involved—but just as quickly as it flared, it fizzled, making us female Marines painfully aware that nothing had changed. We are still unprotected; these are the men that women are supposed to travel overseas with and trust as brothers to have their backs. But there is no trust, just as there will never be true discipline for our "brothers" who violate us, because, well, men are in charge of everything. We women understand instinctively that we need to get in where we fit in—juggling motherhood, being wives, maintaining the household, and doing our jobs with nary a complaint. It was an imbalance that kept us feeling like, really, we weren't part of the family. The Marine Corps is a brotherhood, sure, but we women are not brothers. And therein lies the problem.

Though my experience with the all-male (save for me) squad in Iraq was positive, I did witness a few incidents when fellow female Marines were wrongfully maligned for being women. In one instance, a fellow Marine, a woman, gave me a screenshot of a woman in the Marine Corps who'd taken out all her braids and was rocking her natural afro. Beneath her picture, she was being called everything from a "monkey" to "nappy headed," with male Marines asking, "Why the hell is *that* protecting my country?" and "Why is *that* wearing my uniform?"

Upset, a fellow gunnery sergeant and I took the picture and comments straight to my lieutenant colonel, a black man from Chicago with much more power than I had, fully expecting that he would be equally incensed, take down the names of the men who'd made the comments, and send them to command so that they could be properly disciplined. His response? "She should have worn makeup," he said, shrugging lazily at the papers I'd just finished waving in his face.

I was stunned.

Two decades of that kind of behavior can break the human spirit. But I'm not easily broken.

MY BIG TV BREAK CAME IN A RANDOM, vague email sent to my Operation Heroes Connect account. The person who'd sent it presented the offer to be a mentor representing the Marine Corps as "an amazing opportunity"—without actually mentioning the show. Of course, I read the email and wrote it off as spam, like it was a "cousin" from Timbuktu writing me one of those fraud letters asking for $10,000 to get out of jail. I couldn't close it quick enough.

Two days later, though, I reread it and got a little curious, then sent a response email a day after that. "Can you tell me more?" I asked simply, adding my telephone number to have an actual conversation. A producer called almost immediately and gave me the rundown: impressed with my nonprofit work detailed in several media outlets, they thought I'd be the perfect fit for a new reality show that would have four mentors—one from each military branch—doing on-air service projects for veterans, from building wheelchair ramps for Marines injured while serving to planning the perfect wedding for fellow servicemen. A Skype interview and a few more phone calls later, and I was cleared to star in the pilot of what would eventually turn out to be *American Grit*, a reality show that pit four teams, each led by a military veteran, against each other as they went through a series of military training–style challenges testing their endurance and survival skills in the wilderness.

I was excited about the opportunity—thrilled, really—but I knew it would conflict with my service in the Marine Corps, where I was facing off against two officers whose soul-crushing management style had me on the ropes. I'd already been contemplating retirement, but it was a conversation with a fellow Marine that made clear that I needed to go with my gut: "This is the issue you have," he said. "You're at a point in your career where you are bigger than the Marine Corps, because of the things you're doing outside of the Marine Corps. The people in charge of you do not like that because they can't control that or you."

He was right, and I knew it, although a part of me tried to deny it. The day I got word I was chosen for the pilot, the same commanding officer who'd been so outspoken months before about the Charlotte church shooting that killed nine people was quick to question why I was on the show. As hard as it was not to be stung in that moment, it was even harder not to lose my bearing and respond back. But being on the show would finally give me my voice.

Freedom of speech is a tricky, slippery thing when one is wearing the uniform; we fight for democracy and all that entails, including our right to raise our voices on issues that affect us personally and as a society, but those of us who are doing the fighting aren't allowed to partake in the very thing we're fighting for. We can share our little opinions with our families behind four walls of our personal homes, but we couldn't talk about anything of substance at work; there were no watercooler talks about politics like the ones civilians tend to have at their own jobs.

I cannot and will not dismiss the perks of being in uniform; on some levels, it gives you security. If they're not careful, many will take on this Super Hero complex, not just because of our training and service but also because people revere us as such. If I walk into a restaurant, people are taking pictures, buying rounds, and thanking me for my service; if I wear my uniform to the airport, chances are I'll get upgraded to first class; if I whip out my military ID at a cultural institution, I'll get a military discount—or a free ticket altogether.

When I finally retired, being able to say what was on my mind without fear of repercussions was like breathing fresh air for the first time after being holed up in a windowless room. That's what it felt like—like being in solitary confinement, walled away from the guards, fellow prisoners, family, friends, other humans, with absolutely no one to speak your mind to, complain to, get down to the real issues with, or speak out to about injustices.

Getting out of the military, then, was freedom. Suddenly, I remembered I still had a voice—real things to say—and I felt empowered by that. Getting out just as our country started grappling anew with police brutality and profiling, reproductive rights, gun violence, and more made my exit even sweeter, as now, I'd be able to talk out loud about the issues that mattered to me and that I was grappling with on my own.

This doesn't always go over well for me. I remember a time when, speaking up as a retired Marine, I spoke up about being racially profiled by police—a hot-button topic that became a massive call to action after several high-profile police shootings of unarmed African Americans. I publicly recounted how, as I made my way from California to Virginia for a new post, I was pulled over in Colorado for speeding—even though I was driving slower than the speed limit—and asked gruffly by the state trooper what I was "doing in these parts." I'd also driven Route 66 and stopped in a small Oklahoma town to use the restroom, only to hustle out of the area without having relieved myself out of real fear that the people of the overwhelmingly white enclave were plotting to physically harm me.

Fact: I'm a Marine, but I'm also black, which means that when I'm out of my uniform, I can and have been treated with the same level of disdain and disrespect as any other black person who's faced off against microaggressions and outright racism here in America. Staying silent on this topic and many others denies my humanity, and so I choose to speak up about it—to raise my voice not to add to the noise but in hopes that my personal stories and advocacy will help make a difference.

This makes some people who've come to know me through

my military service nonprofit work or my high-profile gig on *American Grit* feel some type of way. People think that because I'm a black Marine, they're getting another conservative black woman like former Fox news mouthpiece Stacey Dash or reality show star-turned–former Donald Trump White House appointee Omarosa Manigault; they are sadly mistaken and quickly corrected. This plays out often across my social media footprint, particularly on my personal Facebook page, where my posts tend to be unapologetic and public. I've had quite a few people announce they're unfollowing me and are no longer fans because of inane things, such as they are blindly supporting someone who does not have America's best interest in mind or because I have an opinion on a third-rail topic. Some even try to argue before they go, which I don't mind; discourse is a good thing, but what I need them to remember is that as a retired veteran, I'm no longer under a gag order. Retirement has truly allowed me to use my platform and be even more vocal than I was before joining the military. But now I can speak on behalf of those who can't speak because they're still wearing the uniform. On January 20, 2017, I posted on my Facebook the following message: "For all my brothers and sisters still on active duty: don't worry. I'll be your mouthpiece. You may have to watch, but I now have the DD214 and won't let you down."

These sentiments I hold dear, and I'm committed to doing just what I said I would: amplify the voices of the voiceless.

The truth is, speaking your mind and standing your ground comes with significant risk, but also, if done correctly, incredible reward. Here are my top five ways to speak your mind:

1. **Speak with authority and clarity.** Think about what you're going to say before you say it, gather your facts—not alternative facts or opinion but actual truths that can be referenced, corroborated, and serve as sound backup to your theories—and state your case with a clear-eyed, unemotional delivery. This opens the door to your audience actually "hearing" what you have to say, and maybe even coming around to agreeing with you. Remember, opinions are great, but facts are superb.

2. **Develop a thick skin.** Prepare yourself for a warrior who may be every bit as opinionated, outspoken, and clear in battle of words and will. Getting upset and easily insulted by your opponent's presentation of facts, analysis, and opinion or insults won't help you make your point in a disagreement; it only moves him or her closer to the win in an argument. If you give it, be prepared to take it.

3. **Don't be a punk about it.** Some people live to break others down and use their loudest bark to silence others, diminishing their voices and denying their power. Don't shy away: speak up. Use your words as ammunition to shoot down negative talk, and lean on your inner strength and internal fortitude to say exactly what you need to say, when you need to say it. Speaking it makes it easier for you to do it, whatever that "it" is.

4. **Stick to your guns.** Share your opinions with enough people and somebody is bound to feel some way about it. With social media giving people direct access to others and a platform to scream their displeasure to a wide swath of people ready to join them to shoot down "enemies," it's easy to get drowned out by the noise and even intimidated by relentless attacks. Don't bow. Stand tall and firm in your beliefs, argue if you feel like it, or go on ahead and exercise that "block" finger; tune them out on social media, shut off the TV, close the blog and news sites, and get into your "I said what I said"

stance. If someone doesn't like it, that's his or her problem, not yours.

5.   #AllOpinionsDoNotMatter. Sometimes, discouragement comes disguised as concern from people who love and care about us (or at least say that they do). For instance, that voice from my sergeant major, questioning how I managed both my job and my nonprofit while parenting my children, was meant to make me feel bad about the time I spent working on my passion outside of work and home. She did not mean well for me. I didn't tell her how disappointed I was that she, as my mentor, was discouraging me; I simply said, "I can handle it. Don't worry about it." And I continued on with what I wanted to do with my life. You should, too, knowing that every voice that has words for you is not necessarily the voice meant for you to hear. My mother is the one who taught me that. All the time she used to warn me, "It's none of your business what other people think about you," I would argue her down. "What do you mean? Of course it's my business— they're my friends!" I didn't understand what she was telling me until I was much older and wiser. We let other people's opinions of us rule what we do and say and how we move, and we refuse to acknowledge that what others think about you doesn't count anywhere near as much as what *you* think about you. So what if your girlfriend thinks you don't look good in red! If a fabulous red dress caught your eye and you put it on in the dressing room and you liked how the color danced on your skin, why skip buying the dress you like because someone else doesn't like the color on you? How foolish does that make you look? Know this: the only opinion that matters is your own. Wear the dress. Be a Democrat. Carry the gun if that's what you believe in. Carry the sign and march if that's what you want to do. Start the business of your dreams. The only opinion that matters is your own; put everyone else's out of your mind. When you get to that moment when you care less about what other people think and more about your inner drive and ambition, you win. It becomes less about how people perceive you and more about your own ambitions. That may feel a little selfish, but the only way to get what you want is to be unapologetic about your wants, needs, and desires. People's words can be a disease; they legitimately hurt. Lack of encouragement hurts, too. The only way to let your own opinions and desires remain strong and healthy is to treat their words like a disease. It's your job to shield your opinions and desires from that disease like you would a newborn baby from other people's germs. Cover yourself. Cover your goals. And keep pushing.

WARRIOR WORK

Which of the beliefs and causes you support are nonnegotiable for you? Why?

_____

_____

_____

_____

_____

_____

_____

_____

_____

Living with integrity means that who you appear to be is who you really are. Your beliefs, your values, your commitments—your inner realities—are all reflected in how you live your life on the outside. The more you live as who you truly are, the more peace you will invite into your life.

—BARBARA DE ANGELIS, RELATIONSHIP EXPERT AND AUTHOR

11

DON'T TREAD ON ME: PRACTICE SELF-CARE

THE WARRIOR CODE: PRINCIPLE #11

Be you, love you. All ways, always.

—*ALEXANDRA ELLE, POET AND AUTHOR*

These days, airline travel is no picnic: between the cramped seating, the excessive fees, the delays, the stale, musty air inside the cabins, and the funky attitudes that seem to seep into all too many interactions between airline workers and the clients they're supposed to be serving, even a short plane ride can feel more like a five-day, cross-country trek on a budget bus than the luxury trip flying used to be. It's no wonder, then, that when we passengers finally make it to our seats, we do everything we can to physically disengage: before we even buckle our seat belts, we've pulled out our iPads, books, magazines, headphones, and any other distractions we can think of to disappear into so that we can make it through the ride with a reasonable amount of our sanity intact. So distracted are we that we barely even hear, let alone pay attention to, the flight attendants as they issue directives—"Secure your seat belts," "Put your seat backs into their locked and upright position," "Place your mobile devices in airplane mode," and all that jazz—that we miss the most eloquent metaphor to come in the midst of the most rote instructions to be delivered on the thousands of airplanes taking to the skies each day: how to use oxygen masks in the event of a loss of cabin pressure.

If you are traveling with a child or someone who requires assistance, secure your mask on first, and then assist the other person.

The directive is clear and concise: help yourself before you attempt to help others, as doing so, after all, could save two or more lives, not just your own. The science behind this is clear: passengers who experience a drop in cabin pressure can suffer acute cases of hypoxia, a deficiency of oxygen reaching the brain. When that happens, symptoms take humans down: we can experience blurred or tunnel vision, numbness, nausea, dizziness, fatigue, apprehension, belligerence, euphoria. Eventually, within just a few minutes, we can also lose our ability to place oxygen masks on our own faces, rendering us incapable of saving ourselves, much less our children or another person who may need our help.

I can't help but apply that logic to life outside the airplane, away from oxygen masks. Every day, so many of us push ourselves to the very brink: we beat the sun up in the morning, having had only a few hours' sleep, rush to get everyone around us and ourselves ready for their day, bust our butts at work with few breaks and little recognition, rush back home, wrangle the three-ring circus that is dinner, homework, and getting kids ready for bed while we continue to answer to our bosses, our spouses, our friends, our extended families, our churches and organizations for which we volunteer, our own schooling and entrepreneurial pursuits, and whatever else we get ourselves into without thought for the fact that there are only twenty-four hours in a day to do anything. And we brag about it all through tired, red eyes, laying out that laundry list of daily to-dos as if it's some barometer of success, completely dismissing the fact that we're overloaded, exhausted, and, like a passenger who chose to put the oxygen mask on her child rather than herself, gasping for air.

If we can't breathe, how on earth can we effectively care for others?

These days, this is more important than ever, as politics leaves us not only divided but also angry and easily offended by those whose opinions differ from our own; as news cycles move at a frenetic pace, hyping audiences into rapid-fire responses centered on quick emotion rather than thought-out facts; as our patience with one another grows smaller; and as social media allows us to put our lives on display and covet the sugarcoated imagery others push, in part, to make themselves feel more important. Each of these leads not to better lives but more stress as we try our best to keep up.

It doesn't have to be this way.

That much, I knew—even under what was one of the highest stress points in my life: on the ground in Iraq. The U.S. Marine Corps turns out some of the toughest warriors in the world, but we do our jobs under pressure so extreme, it is hard to even begin to measure the toll it takes on us—body, mind, and spirit. Beyond the heroism, beyond the glory, there are nightmares come to life: bombing, screaming, adrenaline, fear. Death. And we have to work through all of that to get our jobs done. No hesitation. No second-guessing. No matter what. Then come home to our families with the memories of that trauma searing our brains. Record suicide rates and post-traumatic stress reports among those of us who have served are a testament to just how difficult all of this is for any mortal to handle.

While away at war, it was hard to practice self-care: there were twelve-hour work shifts and plenty of work to be done. Plus, we weren't at the spa; we were in the desert, living bare-bones with only what we needed and very few extras when it came to creature comforts. My personal self-care was, as I wrote earlier, always rooted in remembering my big reason for why I needed to make it back home: looking at my daughter's picture provided an instant emotional calm. Talking to my family on the phone or via email also was a form of self-care that carried me through; hearing their voices was a salve for my heart and nerves.

Beyond my familial connections, I found a deep solace in exercising—not for work but for myself. This was true for most of my brothers with whom I was serving. Of course, there weren't any gyms, so we had to make do with what we had. Equipment we used for work and battle became makeshift weights. There was always an opportunity to get in a good cardio workout: jumping jacks and running were my go-tos. Squats, lunges, push-ups, heel raises, and crunches were great for muscle endurance and easy to do most anywhere at any time. It was routine for us to challenge one another to be physically superior; once, a fellow Marine challenged me to a contest to see if I could get a six-pack in six weeks. There was no way I was going to lose those bragging rights; I made a point of doing at least one hundred crunches per day during my work break, and then squeezing in another one hundred crunches per day during my downtime. By six weeks, my abs were cut—and I was proud.

Staying fit as part of my self-care routine continues even to this day. Though I have moments during the year when exercising takes a back seat to work and volunteering, I still maintain a vigorous workout most months of the year. I get my playlist together, I decide what I'll work on for the day— arms, legs, back, chest, abs, a combination of a few—and then I put on my headphones and get to work, quickly getting into a zone that not only kicks my endorphins into gear but also gets me right both physically and mentally. Once I've had my workout, I'm ready for my day—no matter what it brings—because I've taken the time to put the mask on my face first. My self-care is nonnegotiable. Critical.

Following through on putting ourselves first is no easy feat. We'll develop a thousand and one excuses why we can't put ourselves first—there's no time to do what we want, we don't have the money to treat ourselves, our spouses/kids/bosses need us right now. But getting in critical self-care isn't about finding time or being a big spender or asking permission to show up for ourselves; it's about *taking* the time and being unapologetic about doing what nourishes us and helps us grow deep down in our souls—about putting the oxygen masks on our faces so that we can breathe and, in turn, have enough energy to help others. Remember: your self-care is non-negotiable. Has to be. Or you die.

THIRTY WAYS TO PRACTICE SELF-CARE

1. Drink water.

2. Drink wine.

3. Stretch.

4. If you work at a desk, stand up for at least eight minutes of every half hour of sitting, and move around for at least two. Your body will thank you for it.

5. Take up a calming hobby, like crocheting, knitting, or sewing.

6. Play a team sport, and commit to playing in a league.

7. Exercise: lift weights and/or work out on a cardio machine.

8. Go for a stroll in the park.

9. Refresh with a nap.

10. Take a long, candlelit bath.

11. Take the time to watch the sunrise or the sunset.

12. Look in the mirror and say something nice to yourself.

13. Say no. Often. And remember that it's a complete sentence.

14. Eat a healthy, balanced diet that includes lots of fresh vegetables and fruit.

15. Ride a bicycle with the wind.

16. Make a playlist of some of your favorite classic music and listen to it while you do something you love.

17. Dance like no one is watching.

18. Take a social media fast: no stalking anyone else's pages, no posting to your own.

19. Meditate.

20. Have sex.

21. Read a good new book, or revisit a favorite classic.

22. Take a trip with friends—or be really bold and go by yourself.

23. Get a massage.

24. Give yourself a mani/pedi—or go to a spa and let someone else do them.

25. Get a facial.

26. Light a scented candle or heat up essential oils or potpourri.

27. Take a nice hot bath with your favorite scented bubble bath or soap.

28. Deep condition your hair, or better yet, let someone else wash, condition, and style it for you.

29. Plant a garden or keep it simple with a planter or two.

30. Kiss the backs of your hands, the insides of your wrists, and then say it loud: "I'm happy being me."

WARRIOR WORK

List four stress triggers that derail your ability to feel happy and satisfied.

_____

_____

_____

_____

_____

List ten of your favorite ways to practice self-care.

It's not selfish to love yourself, take care of yourself, and
to make your happiness a priority. It's necessary.

—MANDY HALE, AUTHOR AND SELF-HELP GURU